Bison

The YACC-compatible Parser Generator
3 November 1999, Bison Version 1.29

by Charles Donnelly and Richard Stallman

Published by the Free Software Foundation
59 Temple Place, Suite 330
Boston, MA 02111-1307 USA
Printed copies are available from the Free Software Foundation.
ISBN 1-882114-44-2

Cover art by Etienne Suvasa.

Bison

Table of Contents

Introduction 1

Conditions for Using Bison 3

GNU GENERAL PUBLIC LICENSE 5

    Preamble 5
    TERMS AND CONDITIONS FOR COPYING, DISTRIBUTION
        AND MODIFICATION 6
    How to Apply These Terms to Your New Programs 11

1   The Concepts of Bison 13

    1.1   Languages and Context-Free Grammars 13
    1.2   From Formal Rules to Bison Input 14
    1.3   Semantic Values 15
    1.4   Semantic Actions 16
    1.5   Bison Output: the Parser File 16
    1.6   Stages in Using Bison 17
    1.7   The Overall Layout of a Bison Grammar 18

2   Examples 19

    2.1   Reverse Polish Notation Calculator 19
        2.1.1   Declarations for rpcalc 19
        2.1.2   Grammar Rules for rpcalc 20
            2.1.2.1   Explanation of input 21
            2.1.2.2   Explanation of line 21
            2.1.2.3   Explanation of expr 22
        2.1.3   The rpcalc Lexical Analyzer 22
        2.1.4   The Controlling Function 24
        2.1.5   The Error Reporting Routine 24
        2.1.6   Running Bison to Make the Parser 24
        2.1.7   Compiling the Parser File 25
    2.2   Infix Notation Calculator: calc 25
    2.3   Simple Error Recovery 27
    2.4   Multi-Function Calculator: mfcalc 28
        2.4.1   Declarations for mfcalc 28
        2.4.2   Grammar Rules for mfcalc 29
        2.4.3   The mfcalc Symbol Table 30
    2.5   Exercises 34

3 Bison Grammar Files 35

  3.1   Outline of a Bison Grammar 35
       3.1.1   The C Declarations Section..................... 35
       3.1.2   The Bison Declarations Section 35
       3.1.3   The Grammar Rules Section.................... 35
       3.1.4   The Additional C Code Section................. 36
  3.2   Symbols, Terminal and Nonterminal 36
  3.3   Syntax of Grammar Rules 38
  3.4   Recursive Rules 39
  3.5   Defining Language Semantics 40
       3.5.1   Data Types of Semantic Values................. 40
       3.5.2   More Than One Value Type................... 40
       3.5.3   Actions.. 40
       3.5.4   Data Types of Values in Actions............... 42
       3.5.5   Actions in Mid-Rule 42
  3.6   Bison Declarations 44
       3.6.1   Token Type Names 45
       3.6.2   Operator Precedence........................... 46
       3.6.3   The Collection of Value Types.................. 46
       3.6.4   Nonterminal Symbols.......................... 47
       3.6.5   Suppressing Conflict Warnings.................. 47
       3.6.6   The Start-Symbol 48
       3.6.7   A Pure (Reentrant) Parser 48
       3.6.8   Bison Declaration Summary.................... 48
  3.7   Multiple Parsers in the Same Program 50

4 Parser C-Language Interface 51

  4.1   The Parser Function yyparse 51
  4.2   The Lexical Analyzer Function yylex.................... 51
       4.2.1   Calling Convention for yylex.................. 51
       4.2.2   Semantic Values of Tokens 53
       4.2.3   Textual Positions of Tokens 53
       4.2.4   Calling Conventions for Pure Parsers........... 54
  4.3   The Error Reporting Function yyerror 55
  4.4   Special Features for Use in Actions 56

5 The Bison Parser Algorithm 59

   5.1   Look-Ahead Tokens 59
   5.2   Shift/Reduce Conflicts. 60
   5.3   Operator Precedence 61
       5.3.1   When Precedence is Needed 62
       5.3.2   Specifying Operator Precedence. 62
       5.3.3   Precedence Examples 63
       5.3.4   How Precedence Works 63
   5.4   Context-Dependent Precedence. 63
   5.5   Parser States 64
   5.6   Reduce/Reduce Conflicts 65
   5.7   Mysterious Reduce/Reduce Conflicts. 66
   5.8   Stack Overflow, and How to Avoid It 68

6 Error Recovery 71

7 Handling Context Dependencies 73

   7.1   Semantic Info in Token Types 73
   7.2   Lexical Tie-ins 74
   7.3   Lexical Tie-ins and Error Recovery 75

8 Debugging Your Parser 77

9 Invoking Bison 79

   9.1   Bison Options. 79
   9.2   Environment Variables. 81
   9.3   Option Cross Key 81
   9.4   Invoking Bison under VMS 82

Appendix B   Bison Symbols 83

Appendix B   Glossary 87

Index 91

Introduction

Bison is a general-purpose parser generator that converts a grammar description for an LALR(1) context-free grammar into a C program to parse that grammar. Once you are proficient with Bison, you may use it to develop a wide range of language parsers, from those used in simple desk calculators to complex programming languages.

Bison is upward compatible with Yacc: all properly-written Yacc grammars ought to work with Bison with no change. Anyone familiar with Yacc should be able to use Bison with little trouble. You need to be fluent in C programming in order to use Bison or to understand this manual.

We begin with tutorial chapters that explain the basic concepts of using Bison and show three explained examples, each building on the last. If you don't know Bison or Yacc, start by reading these chapters. Reference chapters follow which describe specific aspects of Bison in detail.

Bison was written primarily by Robert Corbett; Richard Stallman made it Yacc-compatible. Wilfred Hansen of Carnegie Mellon University added multicharacter string literals and other features.

This edition corresponds to version 1.29 of Bison.

Conditions for Using Bison

As of Bison version 1.24, we have changed the distribution terms for **yyparse** to permit using Bison's output in nonfree programs. Formerly, Bison parsers could be used only in programs that were free software.

The other GNU programming tools, such as the GNU C compiler, have never had such a requirement. They could always be used for nonfree software. The reason Bison was different was not due to a special policy decision; it resulted from applying the usual General Public License to all of the Bison source code.

The output of the Bison utility—the Bison parser file—contains a verbatim copy of a sizable piece of Bison, which is the code for the **yyparse** function. (The actions from your grammar are inserted into this function at one point, but the rest of the function is not changed.) When we applied the GPL terms to the code for **yyparse**, the effect was to restrict the use of Bison output to free software.

We didn't change the terms because of sympathy for people who want to make software proprietary. **Software should be free.** But we concluded that limiting Bison's use to free software was doing little to encourage people to make other software free. So we decided to make the practical conditions for using Bison match the practical conditions for using the other GNU tools.

GNU GENERAL PUBLIC LICENSE

Version 2, June 1991

Copyright © 1989, 1991 Free Software Foundation, Inc.
59 Temple Place - Suite 330, Boston, MA 02111-1307, USA

Preamble

The licenses for most software are designed to take away your freedom
to share and change it. By contrast, the GNU General Public License is
intended to guarantee your freedom to share and change free software—to
make sure the software is free for all its users. This General Public License
applies to most of the Free Software Foundation's software and to any other
program whose authors commit to using it. (Some other Free Software
Foundation software is covered by the GNU Library General Public License
instead.) You can apply it to your programs, too.

When we speak of free software, we are referring to freedom, not price.
Our General Public Licenses are designed to make sure that you have the
freedom to distribute copies of free software (and charge for this service if
you wish), that you receive source code or can get it if you want it, that you
can change the software or use pieces of it in new free programs; and that
you know you can do these things.

To protect your rights, we need to make restrictions that forbid anyone to
deny you these rights or to ask you to surrender the rights. These restrictions
translate to certain responsibilities for you if you distribute copies of the
software, or if you modify it.

For example, if you distribute copies of such a program, whether gratis
or for a fee, you must give the recipients all the rights that you have. You
must make sure that they, too, receive or can get the source code. And you
must show them these terms so they know their rights.

We protect your rights with two steps: (1) copyright the software, and
(2) offer you this license which gives you legal permission to copy, distribute
and/or modify the software.

Also, for each author's protection and ours, we want to make certain
that everyone understands that there is no warranty for this free software.
If the software is modified by someone else and passed on, we want its recipients to know that what they have is not the original, so that any problems
introduced by others will not reflect on the original authors' reputations.

Finally, any free program is threatened constantly by software patents.
We wish to avoid the danger that redistributors of a free program will in-
dividually obtain patent licenses, in effect making the program proprietary.

To prevent this, we have made it clear that any patent must be licensed for everyone's free use or not licensed at all.

The precise terms and conditions for copying, distribution and modification follow.

TERMS AND CONDITIONS FOR COPYING, DISTRIBUTION AND MODIFICATION

0. This License applies to any program or other work which contains a notice placed by the copyright holder saying it may be distributed under the terms of this General Public License. The "Program", below, refers to any such program or work, and a "work based on the Program" means either the Program or any derivative work under copyright law: that is to say, a work containing the Program or a portion of it, either verbatim or with modifications and/or translated into another language. (Hereinafter, translation is included without limitation in the term "modification".) Each licensee is addressed as "you".

   Activities other than copying, distribution and modification are not covered by this License; they are outside its scope. The act of running the Program is not restricted, and the output from the Program is covered only if its contents constitute a work based on the Program (independent of having been made by running the Program). Whether that is true depends on what the Program does.

1. You may copy and distribute verbatim copies of the Program's source code as you receive it, in any medium, provided that you conspicuously and appropriately publish on each copy an appropriate copyright notice and disclaimer of warranty; keep intact all the notices that refer to this License and to the absence of any warranty; and give any other recipients of the Program a copy of this License along with the Program.

   You may charge a fee for the physical act of transferring a copy, and you may at your option offer warranty protection in exchange for a fee.

2. You may modify your copy or copies of the Program or any portion of it, thus forming a work based on the Program, and copy and distribute such modifications or work under the terms of Section 1 above, provided that you also meet all of these conditions:

   a. You must cause the modified files to carry prominent notices stating that you changed the files and the date of any change.

   b. You must cause any work that you distribute or publish, that in whole or in part contains or is derived from the Program or any part thereof, to be licensed as a whole at no charge to all third parties under the terms of this License.

   c. If the modified program normally reads commands interactively when run, you must cause it, when started running for such interactive use in the most ordinary way, to print or display an announcement including an appropriate copyright notice and a notice that there is no warranty (or else, saying that you provide a warranty) and that users may redistribute the program under these conditions, and telling the user how to view a copy of this License. (Exception: if the Program itself is interactive but does not normally print such an announcement, your work based on the Program is not required to print an announcement.)

These requirements apply to the modified work as a whole. If identifiable sections of that work are not derived from the Program, and can be reasonably considered independent and separate works in themselves, then this License, and its terms, do not apply to those sections when you distribute them as separate works. But when you distribute the same sections as part of a whole which is a work based on the Program, the distribution of the whole must be on the terms of this License, whose permissions for other licensees extend to the entire whole, and thus to each and every part regardless of who wrote it.

Thus, it is not the intent of this section to claim rights or contest your rights to work written entirely by you; rather, the intent is to exercise the right to control the distribution of derivative or collective works based on the Program.

In addition, mere aggregation of another work not based on the Program with the Program (or with a work based on the Program) on a volume of a storage or distribution medium does not bring the other work under the scope of this License.

3. You may copy and distribute the Program (or a work based on it, under Section 2) in object code or executable form under the terms of Sections 1 and 2 above provided that you also do one of the following:

   a. Accompany it with the complete corresponding machine-readable source code, which must be distributed under the terms of Sections 1 and 2 above on a medium customarily used for software interchange; or,

   b. Accompany it with a written offer, valid for at least three years, to give any third party, for a charge no more than your cost of physically performing source distribution, a complete machine-readable copy of the corresponding source code, to be distributed under the terms of Sections 1 and 2 above on a medium customarily used for software interchange; or,

   c. Accompany it with the information you received as to the offer to distribute corresponding source code. (This alternative is allowed only for noncommercial distribution and only if you received the program in object code or executable form with such an offer, in accord with Subsection b above.)

The source code for a work means the preferred form of the work for making modifications to it. For an executable work, complete source code means all the source code for all modules it contains, plus any associated interface definition files, plus the scripts used to control compilation and installation of the executable. However, as a special exception, the source code distributed need not include anything that is normally distributed (in either source or binary form) with the major components (compiler, kernel, and so on) of the operating system on which the executable runs, unless that component itself accompanies the executable.

If distribution of executable or object code is made by offering access to copy from a designated place, then offering equivalent access to copy the source code from the same place counts as distribution of the source code, even though third parties are not compelled to copy the source along with the object code.

4. You may not copy, modify, sublicense, or distribute the Program except as expressly provided under this License. Any attempt otherwise to copy, modify, sublicense or distribute the Program is void, and will automatically terminate your rights under this License. However, parties who have received copies, or rights, from you under this License will not have their licenses terminated so long as such parties remain in full compliance.

5. You are not required to accept this License, since you have not signed it. However, nothing else grants you permission to modify or distribute the Program or its derivative works. These actions are prohibited by law if you do not accept this License. Therefore, by modifying or distributing the Program (or any work based on the Program), you indicate your acceptance of this License to do so, and all its terms and conditions for copying, distributing or modifying the Program or works based on it.

6. Each time you redistribute the Program (or any work based on the Program), the recipient automatically receives a license from the original licensor to copy, distribute or modify the Program subject to these terms and conditions. You may not impose any further restrictions on the recipients' exercise of the rights granted herein. You are not responsible for enforcing compliance by third parties to this License.

7. If, as a consequence of a court judgment or allegation of patent infringement or for any other reason (not limited to patent issues), conditions are imposed on you (whether by court order, agreement or otherwise) that contradict the conditions of this License, they do not excuse you from the conditions of this License. If you cannot distribute so as to satisfy simultaneously your obligations under this License and any other pertinent obligations, then as a consequence you may not distribute the Program at all. For example, if a patent license would not permit royalty-free redistribution of the Program by all those who receive copies directly or indirectly through you, then the only way you could satisfy both it and this License would be to refrain entirely from distribution of the Program.

If any portion of this section is held invalid or unenforceable under any particular circumstance, the balance of the section is intended to apply and the section as a whole is intended to apply in other circumstances.

It is not the purpose of this section to induce you to infringe any patents or other property right claims or to contest validity of any such claims; this section has the sole purpose of protecting the integrity of the free software distribution system, which is implemented by public license practices. Many people have made generous contributions to the wide range of software distributed through that system in reliance on consistent application of that system; it is up to the author/donor to decide if he or she is willing to distribute software through any other system and a licensee cannot impose that choice.

This section is intended to make thoroughly clear what is believed to be a consequence of the rest of this License.

8. If the distribution and/or use of the Program is restricted in certain countries either by patents or by copyrighted interfaces, the original copyright holder who places the Program under this License may add an explicit geographical distribution limitation excluding those countries, so that distribution is permitted only in or among countries not thus excluded. In such case, this License incorporates the limitation as if written in the body of this License.

9. The Free Software Foundation may publish revised and/or new versions of the General Public License from time to time. Such new versions will be similar in spirit to the present version, but may differ in detail to address new problems or concerns.

Each version is given a distinguishing version number. If the Program specifies a version number of this License which applies to it and "any later version", you have the option of following the terms and conditions either of that version or of any later version published by the Free Software Foundation. If the Program does not specify a version number of this License, you may choose any version ever published by the Free Software Foundation.

10. If you wish to incorporate parts of the Program into other free programs whose distribution conditions are different, write to the author to ask for permission. For software which is copyrighted by the Free Software Foundation, write to the Free Software Foundation; we sometimes make exceptions for this. Our decision will be guided by the two goals of preserving the free status of all derivatives of our free software and of promoting the sharing and reuse of software generally.

NO WARRANTY

11. BECAUSE THE PROGRAM IS LICENSED FREE OF CHARGE, THERE IS NO WARRANTY FOR THE PROGRAM, TO THE EXTENT PERMITTED BY APPLICABLE LAW. EXCEPT WHEN

OTHERWISE STATED IN WRITING THE COPYRIGHT HOLDERS AND/OR OTHER PARTIES PROVIDE THE PROGRAM "AS IS" WITHOUT WARRANTY OF ANY KIND, EITHER EXPRESSED OR IMPLIED, INCLUDING, BUT NOT LIMITED TO, THE IMPLIED WARRANTIES OF MERCHANTABILITY AND FITNESS FOR A PARTICULAR PURPOSE. THE ENTIRE RISK AS TO THE QUALITY AND PERFORMANCE OF THE PROGRAM IS WITH YOU. SHOULD THE PROGRAM PROVE DEFECTIVE, YOU ASSUME THE COST OF ALL NECESSARY SERVICING, REPAIR OR CORRECTION.

12. IN NO EVENT UNLESS REQUIRED BY APPLICABLE LAW OR AGREED TO IN WRITING WILL ANY COPYRIGHT HOLDER, OR ANY OTHER PARTY WHO MAY MODIFY AND/OR REDISTRIBUTE THE PROGRAM AS PERMITTED ABOVE, BE LIABLE TO YOU FOR DAMAGES, INCLUDING ANY GENERAL, SPECIAL, INCIDENTAL OR CONSEQUENTIAL DAMAGES ARISING OUT OF THE USE OR INABILITY TO USE THE PROGRAM (INCLUDING BUT NOT LIMITED TO LOSS OF DATA OR DATA BEING RENDERED INACCURATE OR LOSSES SUSTAINED BY YOU OR THIRD PARTIES OR A FAILURE OF THE PROGRAM TO OPERATE WITH ANY OTHER PROGRAMS), EVEN IF SUCH HOLDER OR OTHER PARTY HAS BEEN ADVISED OF THE POSSIBILITY OF SUCH DAMAGES.

END OF TERMS AND CONDITIONS

How to Apply These Terms to Your New Programs

If you develop a new program, and you want it to be of the greatest possible use to the public, the best way to achieve this is to make it free software which everyone can redistribute and change under these terms.

To do so, attach the following notices to the program. It is safest to attach them to the start of each source file to most effectively convey the exclusion of warranty; and each file should have at least the "copyright" line and a pointer to where the full notice is found.

> *one line to give the program's name and a brief idea of what it does.*
> Copyright (C) 19yy *name of author*
>
> This program is free software; you can redistribute it and/or modify
> it under the terms of the GNU General Public License as published by
> the Free Software Foundation; either version 2 of the License, or
> (at your option) any later version.
>
> This program is distributed in the hope that it will be useful,
> but WITHOUT ANY WARRANTY; without even the implied warranty of
> MERCHANTABILITY or FITNESS FOR A PARTICULAR PURPOSE. See the
> GNU General Public License for more details.
>
> You should have received a copy of the GNU General Public License
> along with this program; if not, write to the Free Software
> Foundation, Inc., 59 Temple Place - Suite 330,
> Boston, MA 02111-1307, USA.

Also add information on how to contact you by electronic and paper mail.

If the program is interactive, make it output a short notice like this when it starts in an interactive mode:

> Gnomovision version 69, Copyright (C) 19yy *name of author*
> Gnomovision comes with ABSOLUTELY NO WARRANTY; for details
> type 'show w'.
> This is free software, and you are welcome to redistribute it
> under certain conditions; type 'show c' for details.

The hypothetical commands 'show w' and 'show c' should show the appropriate parts of the General Public License. Of course, the commands you use may be called something other than 'show w' and 'show c'; they could even be mouse-clicks or menu items—whatever suits your program.

You should also get your employer (if you work as a programmer) or your school, if any, to sign a "copyright disclaimer" for the program, if necessary. Here is a sample; alter the names:

> Yoyodyne, Inc., hereby disclaims all copyright interest in the program
> 'Gnomovision' (which makes passes at compilers) written by James Hacker.

signature of Ty Coon, 1 April 1989

Ty Coon, President of Vice

This General Public License does not permit incorporating your program into proprietary programs. If your program is a subroutine library, you may consider it more useful to permit linking proprietary applications with the library. If this is what you want to do, use the GNU Library General Public License instead of this License.

1 The Concepts of Bison

This chapter introduces many of the basic concepts without which the details of Bison will not make sense. If you do not already know how to use Bison or Yacc, we suggest you start by reading this chapter carefully.

1.1 Languages and Context-Free Grammars

In order for Bison to parse a language, it must be described by a *context-free grammar*. This means that you specify one or more *syntactic groupings* and give rules for constructing them from their parts. For example, in the C language, one kind of grouping is called an 'expression'. One rule for making an expression might be, "An expression can be made of a minus sign and another expression". Another would be, "An expression can be an integer". As you can see, rules are often recursive, but there must be at least one rule which leads out of the recursion.

The most common formal system for presenting such rules for humans to read is *Backus-Naur Form* or "BNF", which was developed in order to specify the language Algol 60. Any grammar expressed in BNF is a context-free grammar. The input to Bison is essentially machine-readable BNF.

Not all context-free languages can be handled by Bison, only those that are LALR(1). In brief, this means that it must be possible to tell how to parse any portion of an input string with just a single token of look-ahead. Strictly speaking, that is a description of an LR(1) grammar, and LALR(1) involves additional restrictions that are hard to explain simply; but it is rare in actual practice to find an LR(1) grammar that fails to be LALR(1). See Section 5.7 [Mysterious Reduce/Reduce Conflicts], page 66, for more information on this.

In the formal grammatical rules for a language, each kind of syntactic unit or grouping is named by a *symbol*. Those which are built by grouping smaller constructs according to grammatical rules are called *nonterminal symbols*; those which can't be subdivided are called *terminal symbols* or *token types*. We call a piece of input corresponding to a single terminal symbol a *token*, and a piece corresponding to a single nonterminal symbol a *grouping*.

We can use the C language as an example of what symbols, terminal and nonterminal, mean. The tokens of C are identifiers, constants (numeric and string), and the various keywords, arithmetic operators and punctuation marks. So the terminal symbols of a grammar for C include 'identifier', 'number', 'string', plus one symbol for each keyword, operator or punctuation mark: 'if', 'return', 'const', 'static', 'int', 'char', 'plus-sign', 'open-brace', 'close-brace', 'comma' and many more. (These tokens can be subdivided into characters, but that is a matter of lexicography, not grammar.)

Here is a simple C function subdivided into tokens:

```
int                 /* keyword 'int' */
square (x)          /* identifier, open-paren, */
                    /* identifier, close-paren */
    int x;          /* keyword 'int', identifier, semicolon */
{                   /* open-brace */
  return x * x;     /* keyword 'return', identifier, */
                    /* asterisk, identifier, semicolon */
}                   /* close-brace */
```

The syntactic groupings of C include the expression, the statement, the declaration, and the function definition. These are represented in the grammar of C by nonterminal symbols 'expression', 'statement', 'declaration' and 'function definition'. The full grammar uses dozens of additional language constructs, each with its own nonterminal symbol, in order to express the meanings of these four. The example above is a function definition; it contains one declaration, and one statement. In the statement, each 'x' is an expression and so is 'x * x'.

Each nonterminal symbol must have grammatical rules showing how it is made out of simpler constructs. For example, one kind of C statement is the **return** statement; this would be described with a grammar rule which reads informally as follows:

A 'statement' can be made of a 'return' keyword, an 'expression' and a 'semicolon'.

There would be many other rules for 'statement', one for each kind of statement in C.

One nonterminal symbol must be distinguished as the special one which defines a complete utterance in the language. It is called the *start symbol*. In a compiler, this means a complete input program. In the C language, the nonterminal symbol 'sequence of definitions and declarations' plays this role.

For example, '1 + 2' is a valid C expression—a valid part of a C program— but it is not valid as an *entire* C program. In the context-free grammar of C, this follows from the fact that 'expression' is not the start symbol.

The Bison parser reads a sequence of tokens as its input, and groups the tokens using the grammar rules. If the input is valid, the end result is that the entire token sequence reduces to a single grouping whose symbol is the grammar's start symbol. If we use a grammar for C, the entire input must be a 'sequence of definitions and declarations'. If not, the parser reports a syntax error.

1.2 From Formal Rules to Bison Input

A formal grammar is a mathematical construct. To define the language for Bison, you must write a file expressing the grammar in Bison syntax: a *Bison grammar* file. See Chapter 3 [Bison Grammar Files], page 35.

A nonterminal symbol in the formal grammar is represented in Bison input as an identifier, like an identifier in C. By convention, it should be in lower case, such as `expr`, `stmt` or `declaration`.

The Bison representation for a terminal symbol is also called a *token type*. Token types as well can be represented as C-like identifiers. By convention, these identifiers should be upper case to distinguish them from nonterminals: for example, `INTEGER`, `IDENTIFIER`, `IF` or `RETURN`. A terminal symbol that stands for a particular keyword in the language should be named after that keyword converted to upper case. The terminal symbol `error` is reserved for error recovery. See Section 3.2 [Symbols], page 36.

A terminal symbol can also be represented as a character literal, just like a C character constant. You should do this whenever a token is just a single character (parenthesis, plus-sign, etc.): use that same character in a literal as the terminal symbol for that token.

A third way to represent a terminal symbol is with a C string constant containing several characters. See Section 3.2 [Symbols], page 36, for more information.

The grammar rules also have an expression in Bison syntax. For example, here is the Bison rule for a C `return` statement. The semicolon in quotes is a literal character token, representing part of the C syntax for the statement; the naked semicolon, and the colon, are Bison punctuation used in every rule.

```
stmt:    RETURN expr ';'
         ;
```

See Section 3.3 [Syntax of Grammar Rules], page 38.

1.3 Semantic Values

A formal grammar selects tokens only by their classifications: for example, if a rule mentions the terminal symbol 'integer constant', it means that *any* integer constant is grammatically valid in that position. The precise value of the constant is irrelevant to how to parse the input: if 'x+4' is grammatical then 'x+1' or 'x+3989' is equally grammatical.

But the precise value is very important for what the input means once it is parsed. A compiler is useless if it fails to distinguish between 4, 1 and 3989 as constants in the program! Therefore, each token in a Bison grammar has both a token type and a *semantic value*. See Section 3.5 [Defining Language Semantics], page 40, for details.

The token type is a terminal symbol defined in the grammar, such as `INTEGER`, `IDENTIFIER` or `','`. It tells everything you need to know to decide where the token may validly appear and how to group it with other tokens. The grammar rules know nothing about tokens except their types.

The semantic value has all the rest of the information about the meaning of the token, such as the value of an integer, or the name of an identifier.

(A token such as ',' which is just punctuation doesn't need to have any semantic value.)

For example, an input token might be classified as token type INTEGER and have the semantic value 4. Another input token might have the same token type INTEGER but value 3989. When a grammar rule says that INTEGER is allowed, either of these tokens is acceptable because each is an INTEGER. When the parser accepts the token, it keeps track of the token's semantic value.

Each grouping can also have a semantic value as well as its nonterminal symbol. For example, in a calculator, an expression typically has a semantic value that is a number. In a compiler for a programming language, an expression typically has a semantic value that is a tree structure describing the meaning of the expression.

1.4 Semantic Actions

In order to be useful, a program must do more than parse input; it must also produce some output based on the input. In a Bison grammar, a grammar rule can have an *action* made up of C statements. Each time the parser recognizes a match for that rule, the action is executed. See Section 3.5.3 [Actions], page 40.

Most of the time, the purpose of an action is to compute the semantic value of the whole construct from the semantic values of its parts. For example, suppose we have a rule which says an expression can be the sum of two expressions. When the parser recognizes such a sum, each of the subexpressions has a semantic value which describes how it was built up. The action for this rule should create a similar sort of value for the newly recognized larger expression.

For example, here is a rule that says an expression can be the sum of two subexpressions:

```
expr: expr '+' expr   { $$ = $1 + $3; }
    ;
```

The action says how to produce the semantic value of the sum expression from the values of the two subexpressions.

1.5 Bison Output: the Parser File

When you run Bison, you give it a Bison grammar file as input. The output is a C source file that parses the language described by the grammar. This file is called a *Bison parser*. Keep in mind that the Bison utility and the Bison parser are two distinct programs: the Bison utility is a program whose output is the Bison parser that becomes part of your program.

The job of the Bison parser is to group tokens into groupings according to the grammar rules—for example, to build identifiers and operators into expressions. As it does this, it runs the actions for the grammar rules it uses.

The tokens come from a function called the *lexical analyzer* that you must supply in some fashion (such as by writing it in C). The Bison parser calls the lexical analyzer each time it wants a new token. It doesn't know what is "inside" the tokens (though their semantic values may reflect this). Typically the lexical analyzer makes the tokens by parsing characters of text, but Bison does not depend on this. See Section 4.2 [The Lexical Analyzer Function `yylex`], page 51.

The Bison parser file is C code which defines a function named `yyparse` which implements that grammar. This function does not make a complete C program: you must supply some additional functions. One is the lexical analyzer. Another is an error-reporting function which the parser calls to report an error. In addition, a complete C program must start with a function called `main`; you have to provide this, and arrange for it to call `yyparse` or the parser will never run. See Chapter 4 [Parser C-Language Interface], page 51.

Aside from the token type names and the symbols in the actions you write, all variable and function names used in the Bison parser file begin with 'yy' or 'YY'. This includes interface functions such as the lexical analyzer function `yylex`, the error reporting function `yyerror` and the parser function `yyparse` itself. This also includes numerous identifiers used for internal purposes. Therefore, you should avoid using C identifiers starting with 'yy' or 'YY' in the Bison grammar file except for the ones defined in this manual.

1.6 Stages in Using Bison

The actual language-design process using Bison, from grammar specification to a working compiler or interpreter, has these parts:

1. Formally specify the grammar in a form recognized by Bison (see Chapter 3 [Bison Grammar Files], page 35). For each grammatical rule in the language, describe the action that is to be taken when an instance of that rule is recognized. The action is described by a sequence of C statements.

2. Write a lexical analyzer to process input and pass tokens to the parser. The lexical analyzer may be written by hand in C (see Section 4.2 [The Lexical Analyzer Function `yylex`], page 51). It could also be produced using Lex, but the use of Lex is not discussed in this manual.

3. Write a controlling function that calls the Bison-produced parser.

4. Write error-reporting routines.

To turn this source code as written into a runnable program, you must follow these steps:

1. Run Bison on the grammar to produce the parser.

2. Compile the code output by Bison, as well as any other source files.

3. Link the object files to produce the finished product.

1.7 The Overall Layout of a Bison Grammar

The input file for the Bison utility is a *Bison grammar file*. The general form of a Bison grammar file is as follows:

```
%{
C declarations
%}

Bison declarations

%%
Grammar rules
%%
Additional C code
```

The '%%', '%{' and '%}' are punctuation that appears in every Bison grammar file to separate the sections.

The C declarations may define types and variables used in the actions. You can also use preprocessor commands to define macros used there, and use `#include` to include header files that do any of these things.

The Bison declarations declare the names of the terminal and nonterminal symbols, and may also describe operator precedence and the data types of semantic values of various symbols.

The grammar rules define how to construct each nonterminal symbol from its parts.

The additional C code can contain any C code you want to use. Often the definition of the lexical analyzer `yylex` goes here, plus subroutines called by the actions in the grammar rules. In a simple program, all the rest of the program can go here.

2 Examples

Now we show and explain three sample programs written using Bison: a reverse polish notation calculator, an algebraic (infix) notation calculator, and a multi-function calculator. All three have been tested under BSD Unix 4.3; each produces a usable, though limited, interactive desk-top calculator.

These examples are simple, but Bison grammars for real programming languages are written the same way.

2.1 Reverse Polish Notation Calculator

The first example is that of a simple double-precision *reverse polish notation* calculator (a calculator using postfix operators). This example provides a good starting point, since operator precedence is not an issue. The second example will illustrate how operator precedence is handled.

The source code for this calculator is named 'rpcalc.y'. The '.y' extension is a convention used for Bison input files.

2.1.1 Declarations for rpcalc

Here are the C and Bison declarations for the reverse polish notation calculator. As in C, comments are placed between '/*...*/'.

```
/* Reverse polish notation calculator. */

%{
#define YYSTYPE double
#include <math.h>
%}

%token NUM

%% /* Grammar rules and actions follow */
```

The C declarations section (see Section 3.1.1 [The C Declarations Section], page 35) contains two preprocessor directives.

The #define directive defines the macro YYSTYPE, thus specifying the C data type for semantic values of both tokens and groupings (see Section 3.5.1 [Data Types of Semantic Values], page 40). The Bison parser will use whatever type YYSTYPE is defined as; if you don't define it, int is the default. Because we specify double, each token and each expression has an associated value, which is a floating point number.

The #include directive is used to declare the exponentiation function pow.

The second section, Bison declarations, provides information to Bison about the token types (see Section 3.1.2 [The Bison Declarations Section],

page 35). Each terminal symbol that is not a single-character literal must
be declared here. (Single-character literals normally don't need to be declared.) In this example, all the arithmetic operators are designated by
single-character literals, so the only terminal symbol that needs to be declared is NUM, the token type for numeric constants.

2.1.2 Grammar Rules for rpcalc

Here are the grammar rules for the reverse polish notation calculator.

```
input:    /* empty */
        | input line
    ;

line:     '\n'
        | exp '\n'  { printf ("\t%.10g\n", $1); }
    ;

exp:      NUM               { $$ = $1;          }
        | exp exp '+'       { $$ = $1 + $2;     }
        | exp exp '-'       { $$ = $1 - $2;     }
        | exp exp '*'       { $$ = $1 * $2;     }
        | exp exp '/'       { $$ = $1 / $2;     }
     /* Exponentiation */
        | exp exp '^'       { $$ = pow ($1, $2); }
     /* Unary minus    */
        | exp 'n'           { $$ = -$1;         }
    ;
%%
```

The groupings of the rpcalc "language" defined here are the expression
(given the name exp), the line of input (line), and the complete input
transcript (input). Each of these nonterminal symbols has several alternate
rules, joined by the '|' punctuator which is read as "or". The following
sections explain what these rules mean.

The semantics of the language is determined by the actions taken when
a grouping is recognized. The actions are the C code that appears inside
braces. See Section 3.5.3 [Actions], page 40.

You must specify these actions in C, but Bison provides the means for
passing semantic values between the rules. In each action, the pseudo-
variable $$ stands for the semantic value for the grouping that the rule
is going to construct. Assigning a value to $$ is the main job of most actions. The semantic values of the components of the rule are referred to as
$1, $2, and so on.

2.1.2.1 Explanation of `input`

Consider the definition of `input`:

```
input:    /* empty */
        | input line
    ;
```

This definition reads as follows: "A complete input is either an empty string, or a complete input followed by an input line". Notice that "complete input" is defined in terms of itself. This definition is said to be *left recursive* since `input` appears always as the leftmost symbol in the sequence. See Section 3.4 [Recursive Rules], page 39.

The first alternative is empty because there are no symbols between the colon and the first '|'; this means that `input` can match an empty string of input (no tokens). We write the rules this way because it is legitimate to type *Ctrl-d* right after you start the calculator. It's conventional to put an empty alternative first and write the comment '/* empty */' in it.

The second alternate rule (`input line`) handles all nontrivial input. It means, "After reading any number of lines, read one more line if possible." The left recursion makes this rule into a loop. Since the first alternative matches empty input, the loop can be executed zero or more times.

The parser function **yyparse** continues to process input until a grammatical error is seen or the lexical analyzer says there are no more input tokens; we will arrange for the latter to happen at end of file.

2.1.2.2 Explanation of `line`

Now consider the definition of `line`:

```
line:     '\n'
        | exp '\n'   { printf ("\t%.10g\n", $1); }
    ;
```

The first alternative is a token which is a newline character; this means that rpcalc accepts a blank line (and ignores it, since there is no action). The second alternative is an expression followed by a newline. This is the alternative that makes rpcalc useful. The semantic value of the **exp** grouping is the value of **$1** because the **exp** in question is the first symbol in the alternative. The action prints this value, which is the result of the computation the user asked for.

This action is unusual because it does not assign a value to **$$**. As a consequence, the semantic value associated with the **line** is uninitialized (its value will be unpredictable). This would be a bug if that value were ever used, but we don't use it: once rpcalc has printed the value of the user's input line, that value is no longer needed.

2.1.2.3 Explanation of `expr`

The `exp` grouping has several rules, one for each kind of expression. The first rule handles the simplest expressions: those that are just numbers. The second handles an addition-expression, which looks like two expressions followed by a plus-sign. The third handles subtraction, and so on.

```
exp:      NUM
    | exp exp '+'      { $$ = $1 + $2;     }
    | exp exp '-'      { $$ = $1 - $2;     }
    ...
    ;
```

We have used '|' to join all the rules for `exp`, but we could equally well have written them separately:

```
exp:      NUM ;
exp:      exp exp '+'      { $$ = $1 + $2;     } ;
exp:      exp exp '-'      { $$ = $1 - $2;     } ;
    ...
```

Most of the rules have actions that compute the value of the expression in terms of the value of its parts. For example, in the rule for addition, `$1` refers to the first component `exp` and `$2` refers to the second one. The third component, `'+'`, has no meaningful associated semantic value, but if it had one you could refer to it as `$3`. When `yyparse` recognizes a sum expression using this rule, the sum of the two subexpressions' values is produced as the value of the entire expression. See Section 3.5.3 [Actions], page 40.

You don't have to give an action for every rule. When a rule has no action, Bison by default copies the value of `$1` into `$$`. This is what happens in the first rule (the one that uses `NUM`).

The formatting shown here is the recommended convention, but Bison does not require it. You can add or change whitespace as much as you wish. For example, this:

```
exp     : NUM | exp exp '+' {$$ = $1 + $2; } | ...
```

means the same thing as this:

```
exp:      NUM
    | exp exp '+'      { $$ = $1 + $2; }
    | ...
```

The latter, however, is much more readable.

2.1.3 The `rpcalc` Lexical Analyzer

The lexical analyzer's job is low-level parsing: converting characters or sequences of characters into tokens. The Bison parser gets its tokens by calling the lexical analyzer. See Section 4.2 [The Lexical Analyzer Function `yylex`], page 51.

Only a simple lexical analyzer is needed for the RPN calculator. This lexical analyzer skips blanks and tabs, then reads in numbers as **double** and returns them as NUM tokens. Any other character that isn't part of a number is a separate token. Note that the token-code for such a single-character token is the character itself.

The return value of the lexical analyzer function is a numeric code which represents a token type. The same text used in Bison rules to stand for this token type is also a C expression for the numeric code for the type. This works in two ways. If the token type is a character literal, then its numeric code is the ASCII code for that character; you can use the same character literal in the lexical analyzer to express the number. If the token type is an identifier, that identifier is defined by Bison as a C macro whose definition is the appropriate number. In this example, therefore, NUM becomes a macro for `yylex` to use.

The semantic value of the token (if it has one) is stored into the global variable `yylval`, which is where the Bison parser will look for it. (The C data type of `yylval` is YYSTYPE, which was defined at the beginning of the grammar; see Section 2.1.1 [Declarations for `rpcalc`], page 19.)

A token type code of zero is returned if the end-of-file is encountered. (Bison recognizes any nonpositive value as indicating the end of the input.)

Here is the code for the lexical analyzer:

```
/* Lexical analyzer returns a double floating point
   number on the stack and the token NUM, or the ASCII
   character read if not a number.  Skips all blanks
   and tabs, returns 0 for EOF. */

#include <ctype.h>
yylex ()
{
  int c;

  /* skip white space  */
  while ((c = getchar ()) == ' ' || c == '\t')
    ;
  /* process numbers   */
  if (c == '.' || isdigit (c))
    {
      ungetc (c, stdin);
      scanf ("%lf", &yylval);
      return NUM;
    }
```

```
    /* return end-of-file */
    if (c == EOF)
      return 0;
    /* return single chars */
    return c;
}
```

2.1.4 The Controlling Function

In keeping with the spirit of this example, the controlling function is kept
to the bare minimum. The only requirement is that it call **yyparse** to start
the process of parsing.

```
main ()
{
  yyparse ();
}
```

2.1.5 The Error Reporting Routine

When **yyparse** detects a syntax error, it calls the error reporting function
yyerror to print an error message (usually but not always **"parse error"**).
It is up to the programmer to supply **yyerror** (see Chapter 4 [Parser C-
Language Interface], page 51), so here is the definition we will use:

```
#include <stdio.h>

yyerror (s)  /* Called by yyparse on error */
     char *s;
{
  printf ("%s\n", s);
}
```

After **yyerror** returns, the Bison parser may recover from the error and
continue parsing if the grammar contains a suitable error rule (see Chapter 6
[Error Recovery], page 71). Otherwise, **yyparse** returns nonzero. We have
not written any error rules in this example, so any invalid input will cause the
calculator program to exit. This is not clean behavior for a real calculator,
but it is adequate for the first example.

2.1.6 Running Bison to Make the Parser

Before running Bison to produce a parser, we need to decide how to
arrange all the source code in one or more source files. For such a simple
example, the easiest thing is to put everything in one file. The definitions of
yylex, **yyerror** and **main** go at the end, in the "additional C code" section of
the file (see Section 1.7 [The Overall Layout of a Bison Grammar], page 18).

For a large project, you would probably have several source files, and use `make` to arrange to recompile them.

With all the source in a single file, you use the following command to convert it into a parser file:

    bison file_name.y

In this example the file was called 'rpcalc.y' (for "Reverse Polish CALCulator"). Bison produces a file named 'file_name.tab.c', removing the '.y' from the original file name. The file output by Bison contains the source code for `yyparse`. The additional functions in the input file (`yylex`, `yyerror` and `main`) are copied verbatim to the output.

2.1.7 Compiling the Parser File

Here is how to compile and run the parser file:

    # List files in current directory.
    % ls
    rpcalc.tab.c   rpcalc.y

    # Compile the Bison parser.
    # '-lm' tells compiler to search math library for pow.
    % cc rpcalc.tab.c -lm -o rpcalc

    # List files again.
    % ls
    rpcalc   rpcalc.tab.c   rpcalc.y

The file 'rpcalc' now contains the executable code. Here is an example session using `rpcalc`.

```
% rpcalc
4 9 +
13
3 7 + 3 4 5 *+-
-13
3 7 + 3 4 5 * + - n        Note the unary minus, 'n'
13
5 6 / 4 n +
-3.166666667
3 4 ^                      Exponentiation
81
^D                         End-of-file indicator
%
```

2.2 Infix Notation Calculator: `calc`

We now modify rpcalc to handle infix operators instead of postfix. Infix notation involves the concept of operator precedence and the need for parentheses nested to arbitrary depth. Here is the Bison code for 'calc.y', an infix desk-top calculator.

```
/* Infix notation calculator--calc */

%{
#define YYSTYPE double
#include <math.h>
%}

/* BISON Declarations */
%token NUM
%left '-' '+'
%left '*' '/'
%left NEG      /* negation--unary minus */
%right '^'     /* exponentiation        */

/* Grammar follows */
%%
input:    /* empty string */
        | input line
;

line:     '\n'
        | exp '\n'  { printf ("\t%.10g\n", $1); }
;

exp:      NUM                { $$ = $1;          }
        | exp '+' exp        { $$ = $1 + $3;     }
        | exp '-' exp        { $$ = $1 - $3;     }
        | exp '*' exp        { $$ = $1 * $3;     }
        | exp '/' exp        { $$ = $1 / $3;     }
        | '-' exp %prec NEG  { $$ = -$2;         }
        | exp '^' exp        { $$ = pow ($1, $3); }
        | '(' exp ')'        { $$ = $2;          }
;
%%
```

The functions yylex, yyerror and main can be the same as before.

There are two important new features shown in this code.

In the second section (Bison declarations), %left declares token types and says they are left-associative operators. The declarations %left and %right (right associativity) take the place of %token which is used to declare a token type name without associativity. (These tokens are single-character literals, which ordinarily don't need to be declared. We declare them here to specify the associativity.)

Operator precedence is determined by the line ordering of the declarations; the higher the line number of the declaration (lower on the page or screen), the higher the precedence. Hence, exponentiation has the highest precedence, unary minus (**NEG**) is next, followed by '*' and '/', and so on. See Section 5.3 [Operator Precedence], page 61.

The other important new feature is the **%prec** in the grammar section for the unary minus operator. The **%prec** simply instructs Bison that the rule '| '-' exp' has the same precedence as **NEG**—in this case the next-to-highest. See Section 5.4 [Context-Dependent Precedence], page 63.

Here is a sample run of 'calc.y':

```
% calc
4 + 4.5 - (34/(8*3+-3))
6.880952381
-56 + 2
-54
3 ^ 2
9
```

2.3 Simple Error Recovery

Up to this point, this manual has not addressed the issue of *error recovery*—how to continue parsing after the parser detects a syntax error. All we have handled is error reporting with **yyerror**. Recall that by default **yyparse** returns after calling **yyerror**. This means that an erroneous input line causes the calculator program to exit. Now we show how to rectify this deficiency.

The Bison language itself includes the reserved word **error**, which may be included in the grammar rules. In the example below it has been added to one of the alternatives for **line**:

```
line:       '\n'
    | exp '\n'   { printf ("\t%.10g\n", $1); }
    | error '\n' { yyerrok;                   }
    ;
```

This addition to the grammar allows for simple error recovery in the event of a parse error. If an expression that cannot be evaluated is read, the error will be recognized by the third rule for **line**, and parsing will continue. (The **yyerror** function is still called upon to print its message as well.) The action executes the statement **yyerrok**, a macro defined automatically by Bison; its meaning is that error recovery is complete (see Chapter 6 [Error Recovery], page 71). Note the difference between **yyerrok** and **yyerror**; neither one is a misprint.

This form of error recovery deals with syntax errors. There are other kinds of errors; for example, division by zero, which raises an exception signal that is normally fatal. A real calculator program must handle this signal and use `longjmp` to return to `main` and resume parsing input lines; it would also have to discard the rest of the current line of input. We won't discuss this issue further because it is not specific to Bison programs.

2.4 Multi-Function Calculator: `mfcalc`

Now that the basics of Bison have been discussed, it is time to move on to a more advanced problem. The above calculators provided only five functions, '+', '−', '*', '/' and '^'. It would be nice to have a calculator that provides other mathematical functions such as `sin`, `cos`, etc.

It is easy to add new operators to the infix calculator as long as they are only single-character literals. The lexical analyzer `yylex` passes back all nonnumber characters as tokens, so new grammar rules suffice for adding a new operator. But we want something more flexible: built-in functions whose syntax has this form:

> *function_name* (*argument*)

At the same time, we will add memory to the calculator, by allowing you to create named variables, store values in them, and use them later. Here is a sample session with the multi-function calculator:

```
% mfcalc
pi = 3.141592653589
3.1415926536
sin(pi)
0.0000000000
alpha = beta1 = 2.3
2.3000000000
alpha
2.3000000000
ln(alpha)
0.8329091229
exp(ln(beta1))
2.3000000000
%
```

Note that multiple assignment and nested function calls are permitted.

2.4.1 Declarations for `mfcalc`

Here are the C and Bison declarations for the multi-function calculator.

```
%{
#include <math.h>  /* For math functions, cos(), sin(), etc. */
#include "calc.h"  /* Contains definition of 'symrec'        */
%}
%union {
double     val;  /* For returning numbers.                   */
```

```
symrec  *tptr;    /* For returning symbol-table pointers      */
}


%token <val>  NUM       /* Simple double precision number   */
%token <tptr> VAR FNCT  /* Variable and Function            */
%type  <val>  exp


%right '='
%left '-' '+'
%left '*' '/'
%left NEG       /* Negation--unary minus */
%right '^'      /* Exponentiation        */


/* Grammar follows */


%%
```

The above grammar introduces only two new features of the Bison language. These features allow semantic values to have various data types (see Section 3.5.2 [More Than One Value Type], page 40).

The %union declaration specifies the entire list of possible types; this is instead of defining YYSTYPE. The allowable types are now double-floats (for exp and NUM) and pointers to entries in the symbol table. See Section 3.6.3 [The Collection of Value Types], page 46.

Since values can now have various types, it is necessary to associate a type with each grammar symbol whose semantic value is used. These symbols are NUM, VAR, FNCT, and exp. Their declarations are augmented with information about their data type (placed between angle brackets).

The Bison construct %type is used for declaring nonterminal symbols, just as %token is used for declaring token types. We have not used %type before because nonterminal symbols are normally declared implicitly by the rules that define them. But exp must be declared explicitly so we can specify its value type. See Section 3.6.4 [Nonterminal Symbols], page 47.

2.4.2 Grammar Rules for mfcalc

Here are the grammar rules for the multi-function calculator. Most of them are copied directly from calc; three rules, those which mention VAR or FNCT, are new.

```
input:   /* empty */
       | input line
    ;


line:
         '\n'
```

```
                | exp '\n'   { printf ("\t%.10g\n", $1); }
                | error '\n' { yyerrok;                 }
       ;

    exp:     NUM                  { $$ = $1;                          }
             | VAR                { $$ = $1->value.var;               }
             | VAR '=' exp        { $$ = $3; $1->value.var = $3;       }
             | FNCT '(' exp ')'   { $$ = (*($1->value.fnctptr))($3);  }
             | exp '+' exp        { $$ = $1 + $3;                     }
             | exp '-' exp        { $$ = $1 - $3;                     }
             | exp '*' exp        { $$ = $1 * $3;                     }
             | exp '/' exp        { $$ = $1 / $3;                     }
             | '-' exp %prec NEG  { $$ = -$2;                         }
             | exp '^' exp        { $$ = pow ($1, $3);                }
             | '(' exp ')'        { $$ = $2;                          }
       ;
    /* End of grammar */
    %%
```

2.4.3 The `mfcalc` Symbol Table

The multi-function calculator requires a symbol table to keep track of the names and meanings of variables and functions. This doesn't affect the grammar rules (except for the actions) or the Bison declarations, but it requires some additional C functions for support.

The symbol table itself consists of a linked list of records. Its definition, which is kept in the header 'calc.h', is as follows. It provides for either functions or variables to be placed in the table.

```
    /* Data type for links in the chain of symbols.    */
    struct symrec
    {
      char *name;  /* name of symbol                     */
      int type;    /* type of symbol: either VAR or FNCT */
      union {
        double var;            /* value of a VAR         */
        double (*fnctptr)();   /* value of a FNCT        */
      } value;
      struct symrec *next;   /* link field             */
    };
```

```
   typedef struct symrec symrec;

   /* The symbol table: a chain of 'struct symrec'.      */
   extern symrec *sym_table;

   symrec *putsym ();
   symrec *getsym ();
```

The new version of main includes a call to init_table, a function that initializes the symbol table. Here it is, and init_table as well:

```
   #include <stdio.h>

   main ()
   {
     init_table ();
     yyparse ();
   }

   yyerror (s)  /* Called by yyparse on error */
        char *s;
   {
     printf ("%s\n", s);
   }

   struct init
   {
     char *fname;
     double (*fnct)();
   };

   struct init arith_fncts[]
     = {
         "sin", sin,
         "cos", cos,
         "atan", atan,
         "ln", log,
         "exp", exp,
         "sqrt", sqrt,
         0, 0
       };

   /* The symbol table: a chain of 'struct symrec'.  */
   symrec *sym_table = (symrec *)0;
```

```
init_table ()   /* puts arithmetic functions in table. */
{
  int i;
  symrec *ptr;
  for (i = 0; arith_fncts[i].fname != 0; i++)
    {
      ptr = putsym (arith_fncts[i].fname, FNCT);
      ptr->value.fnctptr = arith_fncts[i].fnct;
    }
}
```

By simply editing the initialization list and adding the necessary include files, you can add additional functions to the calculator.

Two important functions allow look-up and installation of symbols in the symbol table. The function putsym is passed a name and the type (VAR or FNCT) of the object to be installed. The object is linked to the front of the list, and a pointer to the object is returned. The function getsym is passed the name of the symbol to look up. If found, a pointer to that symbol is returned; otherwise zero is returned.

```
symrec *
putsym (sym_name,sym_type)
     char *sym_name;
     int sym_type;
{
  symrec *ptr;
  ptr = (symrec *) malloc (sizeof (symrec));
  ptr->name = (char *) malloc (strlen (sym_name) + 1);
  strcpy (ptr->name,sym_name);
  ptr->type = sym_type;
  ptr->value.var = 0; /* set value to 0 even if fctn.  */
  ptr->next = (struct symrec *)sym_table;
  sym_table = ptr;
  return ptr;
}

symrec *
getsym (sym_name)
     char *sym_name;
{
  symrec *ptr;
  for (ptr = sym_table; ptr != (symrec *) 0;
       ptr = (symrec *)ptr->next)
    if (strcmp (ptr->name,sym_name) == 0)
      return ptr;
  return 0;
```

```
}
```

The function `yylex` must now recognize variables, numeric values, and the single-character arithmetic operators. Strings of alphanumeric characters with a leading nondigit are recognized as either variables or functions depending on what the symbol table says about them.

The string is passed to `getsym` for look up in the symbol table. If the name appears in the table, a pointer to its location and its type (VAR or FNCT) is returned to `yyparse`. If it is not already in the table, then it is installed as a VAR using `putsym`. Again, a pointer and its type (which must be VAR) is returned to `yyparse`.

No change is needed in the handling of numeric values and arithmetic operators in `yylex`.

```
#include <ctype.h>
yylex ()
{
  int c;

  /* Ignore whitespace, get first nonwhite character.  */
  while ((c = getchar ()) == ' ' || c == '\t');

  if (c == EOF)
    return 0;
  /* Char starts a number => parse the number.          */
  if (c == '.' || isdigit (c))
    {
      ungetc (c, stdin);
      scanf ("%lf", &yylval.val);
      return NUM;
    }
  /* Char starts an identifier => read the name.         */
  if (isalpha (c))
    {
      symrec *s;
      static char *symbuf = 0;
      static int length = 0;
      int i;

      /* Initially make the buffer long enough
         for a 40-character symbol name.  */
      if (length == 0)
        length = 40, symbuf = (char *)malloc (length + 1);

      i = 0;
      do
```

```
        {
          /* If buffer is full, make it bigger.           */
          if (i == length)
            {
              length *= 2;
              symbuf = (char *)realloc (symbuf, length + 1);
            }
          /* Add this character to the buffer.            */
          symbuf[i++] = c;
          /* Get another character.                        */
          c = getchar ();
        }
      while (c != EOF && isalnum (c));

      ungetc (c, stdin);
      symbuf[i] = '\0';

      s = getsym (symbuf);
      if (s == 0)
        s = putsym (symbuf, VAR);
      yylval.tptr = s;
      return s->type;
    }

  /* Any other character is a token by itself.    */
  return c;
}
```

This program is both powerful and flexible. You may easily add new functions, and it is a simple job to modify this code to install predefined variables such as **pi** or **e** as well.

2.5 Exercises

1. Add some new functions from 'math.h' to the initialization list.

2. Add another array that contains constants and their values. Then modify `init_table` to add these constants to the symbol table. It will be easiest to give the constants type **VAR**.

3. Make the program report an error if the user refers to an uninitialized variable in any way except to store a value in it.

3 Bison Grammar Files

Bison takes as input a context-free grammar specification and produces a C-language function that recognizes correct instances of the grammar.

The Bison grammar input file conventionally has a name ending in '.y'.

3.1 Outline of a Bison Grammar

A Bison grammar file has four main sections, shown here with the appropriate delimiters:

```
%{
C declarations
%}

Bison declarations

%%
Grammar rules
%%

Additional C code
```

Comments enclosed in '/* ... */' may appear in any of the sections.

3.1.1 The C Declarations Section

The *C declarations* section contains macro definitions and declarations of functions and variables that are used in the actions in the grammar rules. These are copied to the beginning of the parser file so that they precede the definition of **yyparse**. You can use '#include' to get the declarations from a header file. If you don't need any C declarations, you may omit the '%{' and '%}' delimiters that bracket this section.

3.1.2 The Bison Declarations Section

The *Bison declarations* section contains declarations that define terminal and nonterminal symbols, specify precedence, and so on. In some simple grammars you may not need any declarations. See Section 3.6 [Bison Declarations], page 44.

3.1.3 The Grammar Rules Section

The *grammar rules* section contains one or more Bison grammar rules, and nothing else. See Section 3.3 [Syntax of Grammar Rules], page 38.

There must always be at least one grammar rule, and the first '%%' (which precedes the grammar rules) may never be omitted even if it is the first thing in the file.

3.1.4 The Additional C Code Section

The *additional C code* section is copied verbatim to the end of the parser file, just as the *C declarations* section is copied to the beginning. This is the most convenient place to put anything that you want to have in the parser file but which need not come before the definition of **yyparse**. For example, the definitions of **yylex** and **yyerror** often go here. See Chapter 4 [Parser C-Language Interface], page 51.

If the last section is empty, you may omit the '%%' that separates it from the grammar rules.

The Bison parser itself contains many static variables whose names start with 'yy' and many macros whose names start with 'YY'. It is a good idea to avoid using any such names (except those documented in this manual) in the additional C code section of the grammar file.

3.2 Symbols, Terminal and Nonterminal

Symbols in Bison grammars represent the grammatical classifications of the language.

A *terminal symbol* (also known as a *token type*) represents a class of syntactically equivalent tokens. You use the symbol in grammar rules to mean that a token in that class is allowed. The symbol is represented in the Bison parser by a numeric code, and the **yylex** function returns a token type code to indicate what kind of token has been read. You don't need to know what the code value is; you can use the symbol to stand for it.

A *nonterminal symbol* stands for a class of syntactically equivalent groupings. The symbol name is used in writing grammar rules. By convention, it should be all lower case.

Symbol names can contain letters, digits (not at the beginning), underscores and periods. Periods make sense only in nonterminals.

There are three ways of writing terminal symbols in the grammar:

- A *named token type* is written with an identifier, like an identifier in C. By convention, it should be all upper case. Each such name must be defined with a Bison declaration such as %token. See Section 3.6.1 [Token Type Names], page 45.

- A *character token type* (or *literal character token*) is written in the grammar using the same syntax used in C for character constants; for example, '+' is a character token type. A character token type doesn't need to be declared unless you need to specify its semantic value data type (see Section 3.5.1 [Data Types of Semantic Values], page 40), associativity, or precedence (see Section 5.3 [Operator Precedence], page 61).

By convention, a character token type is used only to represent a token that consists of that particular character. Thus, the token type '+' is used to represent the character '+' as a token. Nothing enforces this convention, but if you depart from it, your program will confuse other readers.

All the usual escape sequences used in character literals in C can be used in Bison as well, but you must not use the null character as a character literal because its ASCII code, zero, is the code `yylex` returns for end-of-input (see Section 4.2.1 [Calling Convention for `yylex`], page 51).

- A *literal string token* is written like a C string constant; for example, "<=" is a literal string token. A literal string token doesn't need to be declared unless you need to specify its semantic value data type (see Section 3.5.1 [Value Type], page 40), associativity, precedence (see Section 5.3 [Precedence], page 61).

You can associate the literal string token with a symbolic name as an alias, using the `%token` declaration (see Section 3.6.1 [Token Declarations], page 45). If you don't do that, the lexical analyzer has to retrieve the token number for the literal string token from the `yytname` table (see Section 4.2.1 [Calling Convention], page 51).

WARNING: literal string tokens do not work in Yacc.

By convention, a literal string token is used only to represent a token that consists of that particular string. Thus, you should use the token type "<=" to represent the string '<=' as a token. Bison does not enforce this convention, but if you depart from it, people who read your program will be confused.

All the escape sequences used in string literals in C can be used in Bison as well. A literal string token must contain two or more characters; for a token containing just one character, use a character token (see above).

How you choose to write a terminal symbol has no effect on its grammatical meaning. That depends only on where it appears in rules and on when the parser function returns that symbol.

The value returned by `yylex` is always one of the terminal symbols (or 0 for end-of-input). Whichever way you write the token type in the grammar rules, you write it the same way in the definition of `yylex`. The numeric code for a character token type is simply the ASCII code for the character, so `yylex` can use the identical character constant to generate the requisite code. Each named token type becomes a C macro in the parser file, so `yylex` can use the name to stand for the code. (This is why periods don't make sense in terminal symbols.) See Section 4.2.1 [Calling Convention for `yylex`], page 51.

If `yylex` is defined in a separate file, you need to arrange for the token-type macro definitions to be available there. Use the '-d' option when you

run Bison, so that it will write these macro definitions into a separate header
file 'name.tab.h' which you can include in the other source files that need
it. See Chapter 9 [Invoking Bison], page 79.

The symbol **error** is a terminal symbol reserved for error recovery (see
Chapter 6 [Error Recovery], page 71); you shouldn't use it for any other
purpose. In particular, **yylex** should never return this value.

3.3 Syntax of Grammar Rules

A Bison grammar rule has the following general form:

result: *components*...
    ;

where *result* is the nonterminal symbol that this rule describes, and *components* are various terminal and nonterminal symbols that are put together
by this rule (see Section 3.2 [Symbols], page 36).

For example,

```
exp:      exp '+' exp
    ;
```

says that two groupings of type **exp**, with a '+' token in between, can be
combined into a larger grouping of type **exp**.

Whitespace in rules is significant only to separate symbols. You can add
extra whitespace as you wish.

Scattered among the components can be *actions* that determine the semantics of the rule. An action looks like this:

{C statements}

Usually there is only one action and it follows the components. See Section 3.5.3 [Actions], page 40.

Multiple rules for the same *result* can be written separately or can be
joined with the vertical-bar character '|' as follows:

result: *rule1-components*...
    | *rule2-components*...
    ...
    ;

They are still considered distinct rules even when joined in this way.

If *components* in a rule is empty, it means that *result* can match the empty
string. For example, here is how to define a comma-separated sequence of
zero or more **exp** groupings:

```
expseq:   /* empty */
    | expseq1
    ;
```

```
expseq1:  exp
        | expseq1 ',' exp
        ;
```

It is customary to write a comment '/* empty */' in each rule with no components.

3.4 Recursive Rules

A rule is called *recursive* when its *result* nonterminal appears also on its right hand side. Nearly all Bison grammars need to use recursion, because that is the only way to define a sequence of any number of a particular thing. Consider this recursive definition of a comma-separated sequence of one or more expressions:

```
expseq1:  exp
        | expseq1 ',' exp
        ;
```

Since the recursive use of expseq1 is the leftmost symbol in the right hand side, we call this *left recursion*. By contrast, here the same construct is defined using *right recursion*:

```
expseq1:  exp
        | exp ',' expseq1
        ;
```

Any kind of sequence can be defined using either left recursion or right recursion, but you should always use left recursion, because it can parse a sequence of any number of elements with bounded stack space. Right recursion uses up space on the Bison stack in proportion to the number of elements in the sequence, because all the elements must be shifted onto the stack before the rule can be applied even once. See Chapter 5 [The Bison Parser Algorithm], page 59, for further explanation of this.

Indirect or *mutual* recursion occurs when the result of the rule does not appear directly on its right hand side, but does appear in rules for other nonterminals which do appear on its right hand side.

For example:

```
expr:     primary
        | primary '+' primary
        ;

primary:  constant
        | '(' expr ')'
        ;
```

defines two mutually-recursive nonterminals, since each refers to the other.

3.5 Defining Language Semantics

The grammar rules for a language determine only the syntax. The semantics are determined by the semantic values associated with various tokens and groupings, and by the actions taken when various groupings are recognized.

For example, the calculator calculates properly because the value associated with each expression is the proper number; it adds properly because the action for the grouping 'x + y' is to add the numbers associated with x and y.

3.5.1 Data Types of Semantic Values

In a simple program it may be sufficient to use the same data type for the semantic values of all language constructs. This was true in the RPN and infix calculator examples (see Section 2.1 [Reverse Polish Notation Calculator], page 19).

Bison's default is to use type `int` for all semantic values. To specify some other type, define YYSTYPE as a macro, like this:

```
#define YYSTYPE double
```

This macro definition must go in the C declarations section of the grammar file (see Section 3.1 [Outline of a Bison Grammar], page 35).

3.5.2 More Than One Value Type

In most programs, you will need different data types for different kinds of tokens and groupings. For example, a numeric constant may need type `int` or `long`, while a string constant needs type `char *`, and an identifier might need a pointer to an entry in the symbol table.

To use more than one data type for semantic values in one parser, Bison requires you to do two things:

- Specify the entire collection of possible data types, with the %union Bison declaration (see Section 3.6.3 [The Collection of Value Types], page 46).

- Choose one of those types for each symbol (terminal or nonterminal) for which semantic values are used. This is done for tokens with the %token Bison declaration (see Section 3.6.1 [Token Type Names], page 45) and for groupings with the %type Bison declaration (see Section 3.6.4 [Nonterminal Symbols], page 47).

3.5.3 Actions

An action accompanies a syntactic rule and contains C code to be executed each time an instance of that rule is recognized. The task of most actions is to compute a semantic value for the grouping built by the rule from the semantic values associated with tokens or smaller groupings.

An action consists of C statements surrounded by braces, much like a compound statement in C. It can be placed at any position in the rule; it is executed at that position. Most rules have just one action at the end of the rule, following all the components. Actions in the middle of a rule are tricky and used only for special purposes (see Section 3.5.5 [Actions in Mid-Rule], page 42).

The C code in an action can refer to the semantic values of the components matched by the rule with the construct $n, which stands for the value of the nth component. The semantic value for the grouping being constructed is $$. (Bison translates both of these constructs into array element references when it copies the actions into the parser file.)

Here is a typical example:

```
exp:     ...
     | exp '+' exp
         { $$ = $1 + $3; }
```

This rule constructs an exp from two smaller exp groupings connected by a plus-sign token. In the action, $1 and $3 refer to the semantic values of the two component exp groupings, which are the first and third symbols on the right hand side of the rule. The sum is stored into $$ so that it becomes the semantic value of the addition-expression just recognized by the rule. If there were a useful semantic value associated with the '+' token, it could be referred to as $2.

If you don't specify an action for a rule, Bison supplies a default: $$ = $1. Thus, the value of the first symbol in the rule becomes the value of the whole rule. Of course, the default rule is valid only if the two data types match. There is no meaningful default action for an empty rule; every empty rule must have an explicit action unless the rule's value does not matter.

$n with n zero or negative is allowed for reference to tokens and groupings on the stack *before* those that match the current rule. This is a very risky practice, and to use it reliably you must be certain of the context in which the rule is applied. Here is a case in which you can use this reliably:

```
foo:      expr bar '+' expr  { ... }
     | expr bar '-' expr  { ... }
     ;

bar:      /* empty */
     { previous_expr = $0; }
     ;
```

As long as bar is used only in the fashion shown here, $0 always refers to the expr which precedes bar in the definition of foo.

3.5.4 Data Types of Values in Actions

If you have chosen a single data type for semantic values, the $$ and $n
constructs always have that data type.

If you have used %union to specify a variety of data types, then you must
declare a choice among these types for each terminal or nonterminal symbol
that can have a semantic value. Then each time you use $$ or $n, its data
type is determined by which symbol it refers to in the rule. In this example,

```
exp:     ...
    | exp '+' exp
        { $$ = $1 + $3; }
```

$1 and $3 refer to instances of exp, so they all have the data type declared
for the nonterminal symbol exp. If $2 were used, it would have the data
type declared for the terminal symbol '+', whatever that might be.

Alternatively, you can specify the data type when you refer to the value,
by inserting '<type>' after the '$' at the beginning of the reference. For
example, if you have defined types as shown here:

```
%union {
    int itype;
    double dtype;
}
```

then you can write $<itype>1 to refer to the first subunit of the rule as an
integer, or $<dtype>1 to refer to it as a double.

3.5.5 Actions in Mid-Rule

Occasionally it is useful to put an action in the middle of a rule. These
actions are written just like usual end-of-rule actions, but they are executed
before the parser even recognizes the following components.

A mid-rule action may refer to the components preceding it using $n, but
it may not refer to subsequent components because it is run before they are
parsed.

The mid-rule action itself counts as one of the components of the rule.
This makes a difference when there is another action later in the same rule
(and usually there is another at the end): you have to count the actions
along with the symbols when working out which number n to use in $n.

The mid-rule action can also have a semantic value. The action can set
its value with an assignment to $$, and actions later in the rule can refer
to the value using $n. Since there is no symbol to name the action, there is
no way to declare a data type for the value in advance, so you must use the
'$<...>' construct to specify a data type each time you refer to this value.

There is no way to set the value of the entire rule with a mid-rule action,
because assignments to $$ do not have that effect. The only way to set the
value for the entire rule is with an ordinary action at the end of the rule.

Here is an example from a hypothetical compiler, handling a `let` statement that looks like '`let (`variable`) `statement' and serves to create a variable named variable temporarily for the duration of statement. To parse this construct, we must put variable into the symbol table while statement is parsed, then remove it afterward. Here is how it is done:

```
stmt:   LET '(' var ')'
                { $<context>$ = push_context ();
                  declare_variable ($3); }
        stmt    { $$ = $6;
                  pop_context ($<context>5); }
```

As soon as '`let (`variable`)`' has been recognized, the first action is run. It saves a copy of the current semantic context (the list of accessible variables) as its semantic value, using alternative **context** in the data-type union. Then it calls `declare_variable` to add the new variable to that list. Once the first action is finished, the embedded statement **stmt** can be parsed. Note that the mid-rule action is component number 5, so the '**stmt**' is component number 6.

After the embedded statement is parsed, its semantic value becomes the value of the entire `let`-statement. Then the semantic value from the earlier action is used to restore the prior list of variables. This removes the temporary `let`-variable from the list so that it won't appear to exist while the rest of the program is parsed.

Taking action before a rule is completely recognized often leads to conflicts since the parser must commit to a parse in order to execute the action. For example, the following two rules, without mid-rule actions, can coexist in a working parser because the parser can shift the open-brace token and look at what follows before deciding whether there is a declaration or not:

```
compound: '{' declarations statements '}'
        | '{' statements '}'
        ;
```

But when we add a mid-rule action as follows, the rules become nonfunctional:

```
compound: { prepare_for_local_variables (); }
          '{' declarations statements '}'
        | '{' statements '}'
        ;
```

Now the parser is forced to decide whether to run the mid-rule action when it has read no farther than the open-brace. In other words, it must commit to using one rule or the other, without sufficient information to do it correctly. (The open-brace token is what is called the look-ahead token at this time, since the parser is still deciding what to do about it. See Section 5.1 [Look-Ahead Tokens], page 59.)

You might think that you could correct the problem by putting identical actions into the two rules, like this:

```
compound: { prepare_for_local_variables (); }
          '{' declarations statements '}'
        | { prepare_for_local_variables (); }
          '{' statements '}'
        ;
```

But this does not help, because Bison does not realize that the two actions
are identical. (Bison never tries to understand the C code in an action.)

If the grammar is such that a declaration can be distinguished from a
statement by the first token (which is true in C), then one solution which
does work is to put the action after the open-brace, like this:

```
compound: '{' { prepare_for_local_variables (); }
          declarations statements '}'
        | '{' statements '}'
        ;
```

Now the first token of the following declaration or statement, which would
in any case tell Bison which rule to use, can still do so.

Another solution is to bury the action inside a nonterminal symbol which
serves as a subroutine:

```
subroutine: /* empty */
            { prepare_for_local_variables (); }
          ;


compound: subroutine
          '{' declarations statements '}'
        | subroutine
          '{' statements '}'
        ;
```

Now Bison can execute the action in the rule for **subroutine** without deciding which rule for **compound** it will eventually use. Note that the action is
now at the end of its rule. Any mid-rule action can be converted to an end-
of-rule action in this way, and this is what Bison actually does to implement
mid-rule actions.

3.6 Bison Declarations

The *Bison declarations* section of a Bison grammar defines the symbols
used in formulating the grammar and the data types of semantic values. See
Section 3.2 [Symbols], page 36.

All token type names (but not single-character literal tokens such as
'+' and '*') must be declared. Nonterminal symbols must be declared
if you need to specify which data type to use for the semantic value (see
Section 3.5.2 [More Than One Value Type], page 40).

The first rule in the file also specifies the start symbol, by default. If you want some other symbol to be the start symbol, you must declare it explicitly (see Section 1.1 [Languages and Context-Free Grammars], page 13).

3.6.1 Token Type Names

The basic way to declare a token type name (terminal symbol) is as follows:

```
%token name
```

Bison will convert this into a #define directive in the parser, so that the function yylex (if it is in this file) can use the name name to stand for this token type's code.

Alternatively, you can use %left, %right, or %nonassoc instead of %token, if you wish to specify associativity and precedence. See Section 3.6.2 [Operator Precedence], page 46.

You can explicitly specify the numeric code for a token type by appending an integer value in the field immediately following the token name:

```
%token NUM 300
```

It is generally best, however, to let Bison choose the numeric codes for all token types. Bison will automatically select codes that don't conflict with each other or with ASCII characters.

In the event that the stack type is a union, you must augment the %token or other token declaration to include the data type alternative delimited by angle-brackets (see Section 3.5.2 [More Than One Value Type], page 40).

For example:

```
%union {                /* define stack type */
  double val;
  symrec *tptr;
}
%token <val> NUM        /* define token NUM and its type */
```

You can associate a literal string token with a token type name by writing the literal string at the end of a %token declaration which declares the name. For example:

```
%token arrow "=>"
```

For example, a grammar for the C language might specify these names with equivalent literal string tokens:

```
%token  <operator>  OR      "||"
%token  <operator>  LE 134  "<="
%left   OR  "<="
```

Once you equate the literal string and the token name, you can use them interchangeably in further declarations or the grammar rules. The yylex function can use the token name or the literal string to obtain the token type code number (see Section 4.2.1 [Calling Convention], page 51).

3.6.2 Operator Precedence

Use the %left, %right or %nonassoc declaration to declare a token and
specify its precedence and associativity, all at once. These are called *precedence declarations*. See Section 5.3 [Operator Precedence], page 61, for
general information on operator precedence.

The syntax of a precedence declaration is the same as that of %token:
either

> %left *symbols*...

or

> %left <*type*> *symbols*...

And indeed any of these declarations serves the purposes of %token. But
in addition, they specify the associativity and relative precedence for all the
symbols:

- The associativity of an operator *op* determines how repeated uses of the
  operator nest: whether '*x op y op z*' is parsed by grouping *x* with *y* first
  or by grouping *y* with *z* first. %left specifies left-associativity (grouping
  x with *y* first) and %right specifies right-associativity (grouping *y* with
  z first). %nonassoc specifies no associativity, which means that '*x op y
  op z*' is considered a syntax error.

- The precedence of an operator determines how it nests with other operators. All the tokens declared in a single precedence declaration have
  equal precedence and nest together according to their associativity.
  When two tokens declared in different precedence declarations associate, the one declared later has the higher precedence and is grouped
  first.

3.6.3 The Collection of Value Types

The %union declaration specifies the entire collection of possible data
types for semantic values. The keyword %union is followed by a pair of
braces containing the same thing that goes inside a union in C.

For example:

```
%union {
  double val;
  symrec *tptr;
}
```

This says that the two alternative types are **double** and **symrec** *. They are
given names **val** and **tptr**; these names are used in the %token and %type
declarations to pick one of the types for a terminal or nonterminal symbol
(see Section 3.6.4 [Nonterminal Symbols], page 47).

Note that, unlike making a **union** declaration in C, you do not write a
semicolon after the closing brace.

3.6.4 Nonterminal Symbols

When you use %union to specify multiple value types, you must declare the value type of each nonterminal symbol for which values are used. This is done with a %type declaration, like this:

    %type <type> nonterminal...

Here *nonterminal* is the name of a nonterminal symbol, and *type* is the name given in the %union to the alternative that you want (see Section 3.6.3 [The Collection of Value Types], page 46). You can give any number of nonterminal symbols in the same %type declaration, if they have the same value type. Use spaces to separate the symbol names.

You can also declare the value type of a terminal symbol. To do this, use the same <type> construction in a declaration for the terminal symbol. All kinds of token declarations allow <type>.

3.6.5 Suppressing Conflict Warnings

Bison normally warns if there are any conflicts in the grammar (see Section 5.2 [Shift/Reduce Conflicts], page 60). but most real grammars have harmless shift/reduce conflicts which are resolved in a predictable way and would be difficult to eliminate. It is desirable to suppress the warning about these conflicts unless the number of conflicts changes. You can do this with the %expect declaration.

The declaration looks like this:

    %expect n

Here *n* is a decimal integer. The declaration says there should be no warning if there are *n* shift/reduce conflicts and no reduce/reduce conflicts. The usual warning is given if there are either more or fewer conflicts, or if there are any reduce/reduce conflicts.

In general, using %expect involves these steps:

- Compile your grammar without %expect. Use the '-v' option to get a verbose list of where the conflicts occur. Bison will also print the number of conflicts.

- Check each of the conflicts to make sure that Bison's default resolution is what you really want. If not, rewrite the grammar and go back to the beginning.

- Add an %expect declaration, copying the number *n* from the number which Bison printed.

Now Bison will stop annoying you about the conflicts you have checked, but it will warn you again if changes in the grammar result in additional conflicts.

3.6.6 The Start-Symbol

Bison assumes by default that the start symbol for the grammar is the first nonterminal specified in the grammar specification section. The programmer may override this restriction with the `%start` declaration as follows:

`%start` *symbol*

3.6.7 A Pure (Reentrant) Parser

A *reentrant* program is one which does not alter in the course of execution; in other words, it consists entirely of *pure* (read-only) code. Reentrancy is important whenever asynchronous execution is possible; for example, a nonreentrant program may not be safe to call from a signal handler. In systems with multiple threads of control, a nonreentrant program must be called only within interlocks.

Normally, Bison generates a parser which is not reentrant. This is suitable for most uses, and it permits compatibility with YACC. (The standard YACC interfaces are inherently nonreentrant, because they use statically allocated variables for communication with `yylex`, including `yylval` and `yylloc`.)

Alternatively, you can generate a pure, reentrant parser. The Bison declaration `%pure_parser` says that you want the parser to be reentrant. It looks like this:

`%pure_parser`

The result is that the communication variables `yylval` and `yylloc` become local variables in `yyparse`, and a different calling convention is used for the lexical analyzer function `yylex`. See Section 4.2.4 [Calling Conventions for Pure Parsers], page 54, for the details of this. The variable `yynerrs` also becomes local in `yyparse` (see Section 4.3 [The Error Reporting Function `yyerror`], page 55). The convention for calling `yyparse` itself is unchanged.

Whether the parser is pure has nothing to do with the grammar rules. You can generate either a pure parser or a nonreentrant parser from any valid grammar.

3.6.8 Bison Declaration Summary

Here is a summary of all Bison declarations:

`%union`   Declare the collection of data types that semantic values may have (see Section 3.6.3 [The Collection of Value Types], page 46).

`%token`   Declare a terminal symbol (token type name) with no precedence or associativity specified (see Section 3.6.1 [Token Type Names], page 45).

`%right`   Declare a terminal symbol (token type name) that is right-associative (see Section 3.6.2 [Operator Precedence], page 46).

%left   Declare a terminal symbol (token type name) that is left-associative (see Section 3.6.2 [Operator Precedence], page 46).

%nonassoc
                 Declare a terminal symbol (token type name) that is nonassociative (using it in a way that would be associative is a syntax error) (see Section 3.6.2 [Operator Precedence], page 46).

%type   Declare the type of semantic values for a nonterminal symbol (see Section 3.6.4 [Nonterminal Symbols], page 47).

%start   Specify the grammar's start symbol (see Section 3.6.6 [The Start-Symbol], page 48).

%expect   Declare the expected number of shift-reduce conflicts (see Section 3.6.5 [Suppressing Conflict Warnings], page 47).

%pure_parser
                 Request a pure (reentrant) parser program (see Section 3.6.7 [A Pure (Reentrant) Parser], page 48).

%no_lines
                 Don't generate any #line preprocessor commands in the parser file. Ordinarily Bison writes these commands in the parser file so that the C compiler and debuggers will associate errors and object code with your source file (the grammar file). This directive causes them to associate errors with the parser file, treating it an independent source file in its own right.

%raw   The output file 'name.h' normally defines the tokens with Yacc-compatible token numbers. If this option is specified, the internal Bison numbers are used instead. (Yacc-compatible numbers start at 257 except for single-character tokens; Bison assigns token numbers sequentially for all tokens starting at 3.)

%token_table
                 Generate an array of token names in the parser file. The name of the array is yytname; yytname[i] is the name of the token whose internal Bison token code number is i. The first three elements of yytname are always "$", "error", and "$illegal"; after these come the symbols defined in the grammar file.

                 For single-character literal tokens and literal string tokens, the name in the table includes the single-quote or double-quote characters: for example, "'+'" is a single-character literal and "\"<=\"" is a literal string token. All the characters of the literal string token appear verbatim in the string found in the table; even double-quote characters are not escaped. For example, if the token consists of three characters '*"*', its string in yytname contains '"*"*"'. (In C, that would be written as "\"*\"*\"").

When you specify %token_table, Bison also generates macro definitions for macros YYNTOKENS, YYNNTS, and YYNRULES, and YYNSTATES:

YYNTOKENS
> The highest token number, plus one.

YYNNTS   The number of nonterminal symbols.

YYNRULES The number of grammar rules,

YYNSTATES
> The number of parser states (see Section 5.5 [Parser States], page 64).

3.7 Multiple Parsers in the Same Program

Most programs that use Bison parse only one language and therefore contain only one Bison parser. But what if you want to parse more than one language with the same program? Then you need to avoid a name conflict between different definitions of yyparse, yylval, and so on.

The easy way to do this is to use the option '-p prefix' (see Chapter 9 [Invoking Bison], page 79). This renames the interface functions and variables of the Bison parser to start with prefix instead of 'yy'. You can use this to give each parser distinct names that do not conflict.

The precise list of symbols renamed is yyparse, yylex, yyerror, yynerrs, yylval, yychar and yydebug. For example, if you use '-p c', the names become cparse, clex, and so on.

All the other variables and macros associated with Bison are not renamed. These others are not global; there is no conflict if the same name is used in different parsers. For example, YYSTYPE is not renamed, but defining this in different ways in different parsers causes no trouble (see Section 3.5.1 [Data Types of Semantic Values], page 40).

The '-p' option works by adding macro definitions to the beginning of the parser source file, defining yyparse as prefixparse, and so on. This effectively substitutes one name for the other in the entire parser file.

4 Parser C-Language Interface

The Bison parser is actually a C function named **yyparse**. Here we describe the interface conventions of **yyparse** and the other functions that it needs to use.

Keep in mind that the parser uses many C identifiers starting with 'yy' and 'YY' for internal purposes. If you use such an identifier (aside from those in this manual) in an action or in additional C code in the grammar file, you are likely to run into trouble.

4.1 The Parser Function yyparse

You call the function **yyparse** to cause parsing to occur. This function reads tokens, executes actions, and ultimately returns when it encounters end-of-input or an unrecoverable syntax error. You can also write an action which directs **yyparse** to return immediately without reading further.

The value returned by **yyparse** is 0 if parsing was successful (return is due to end-of-input).

The value is 1 if parsing failed (return is due to a syntax error).

In an action, you can cause immediate return from **yyparse** by using these macros:

YYACCEPT   Return immediately with value 0 (to report success).

YYABORT   Return immediately with value 1 (to report failure).

4.2 The Lexical Analyzer Function yylex

The *lexical analyzer* function, **yylex**, recognizes tokens from the input stream and returns them to the parser. Bison does not create this function automatically; you must write it so that **yyparse** can call it. The function is sometimes referred to as a lexical scanner.

In simple programs, **yylex** is often defined at the end of the Bison grammar file. If **yylex** is defined in a separate source file, you need to arrange for the token-type macro definitions to be available there. To do this, use the '-d' option when you run Bison, so that it will write these macro definitions into a separate header file '*name*.tab.h' which you can include in the other source files that need it. See Chapter 9 [Invoking Bison], page 79.

4.2.1 Calling Convention for yylex

The value that **yylex** returns must be the numeric code for the type of token it has just found, or 0 for end-of-input.

When a token is referred to in the grammar rules by a name, that name in the parser file becomes a C macro whose definition is the proper numeric

code for that token type. So `yylex` can use the name to indicate that type.
See Section 3.2 [Symbols], page 36.

When a token is referred to in the grammar rules by a character literal,
the numeric code for that character is also the code for the token type. So
`yylex` can simply return that character code. The null character must not be
used this way, because its code is zero and that is what signifies end-of-input.

Here is an example showing these things:

```
yylex ()
{
  ...
  if (c == EOF)      /* Detect end of file. */
    return 0;
  ...
  if (c == '+' || c == '-')
    return c;        /* Assume token type for '+' is '+'. */
  ...
  return INT;        /* Return the type of the token. */
  ...
}
```

This interface has been designed so that the output from the `lex` utility can
be used without change as the definition of `yylex`.

If the grammar uses literal string tokens, there are two ways that `yylex`
can determine the token type codes for them:

- If the grammar defines symbolic token names as aliases for the literal
  string tokens, `yylex` can use these symbolic names like all others. In
  this case, the use of the literal string tokens in the grammar file has no
  effect on `yylex`.

- `yylex` can find the multicharacter token in the `yytname` table. The
  index of the token in the table is the token type's code. The name of
  a multicharacter token is recorded in `yytname` with a double-quote, the
  token's characters, and another double-quote. The token's characters
  are not escaped in any way; they appear verbatim in the contents of the
  string in the table.

  Here's code for looking up a token in `yytname`, assuming that the characters of the token are stored in `token_buffer`.

```
for (i = 0; i < YYNTOKENS; i++)
  {
    if (yytname[i] != 0
        && yytname[i][0] == '"'
        && strncmp (yytname[i] + 1, token_buffer,
                    strlen (token_buffer))
        && yytname[i][strlen (token_buffer) + 1] == '"'
        && yytname[i][strlen (token_buffer) + 2] == 0)
```

```
          break;
     }
```

The yytname table is generated only if you use the %token_table declaration. See Section 3.6.8 [Decl Summary], page 48.

4.2.2 Semantic Values of Tokens

In an ordinary (nonreentrant) parser, the semantic value of the token must be stored into the global variable yylval. When you are using just one data type for semantic values, yylval has that type. Thus, if the type is int (the default), you might write this in yylex:

```
     . . .
     yylval = value;    /* Put value onto Bison stack. */
     return INT;        /* Return the type of the token. */
     . . .
```

When you are using multiple data types, yylval's type is a union made from the %union declaration (see Section 3.6.3 [The Collection of Value Types], page 46). So when you store a token's value, you must use the proper member of the union. If the %union declaration looks like this:

```
%union {
    int intval;
    double val;
    symrec *tptr;
}
```

then the code in yylex might look like this:

```
     . . .
     yylval.intval = value; /* Put value onto Bison stack. */
     return INT;            /* Return the type of the token. */
     . . .
```

4.2.3 Textual Positions of Tokens

If you are using the '@n'-feature (see Section 4.4 [Special Features for Use in Actions], page 56) in actions to keep track of the textual locations of tokens and groupings, then you must provide this information in yylex. The function yyparse expects to find the textual location of a token just parsed in the global variable yylloc. So yylex must store the proper data in that variable. The value of yylloc is a structure and you need only initialize the members that are going to be used by the actions. The four members are called first_line, first_column, last_line and last_column. Note that the use of this feature makes the parser noticeably slower.

The data type of yylloc has the name YYLTYPE.

4.2.4 Calling Conventions for Pure Parsers

When you use the Bison declaration `%pure_parser` to request a pure, reentrant parser, the global communication variables `yylval` and `yylloc` cannot be used. (See Section 3.6.7 [A Pure (Reentrant) Parser], page 48.) In such parsers the two global variables are replaced by pointers passed as arguments to `yylex`. You must declare them as shown here, and pass the information back by storing it through those pointers.

```
yylex (lvalp, llocp)
    YYSTYPE *lvalp;
    YYLTYPE *llocp;
{
    ...
    *lvalp = value;  /* Put value onto Bison stack.  */
    return INT;      /* Return the type of the token.  */
    ...
}
```

If the grammar file does not use the '@' constructs to refer to textual positions, then the type `YYLTYPE` will not be defined. In this case, omit the second argument; `yylex` will be called with only one argument.

If you use a reentrant parser, you can optionally pass additional parameter information to it in a reentrant way. To do so, define the macro `YYPARSE_PARAM` as a variable name. This modifies the `yyparse` function to accept one argument, of type `void *`, with that name.

When you call `yyparse`, pass the address of an object, casting the address to `void *`. The grammar actions can refer to the contents of the object by casting the pointer value back to its proper type and then dereferencing it. Here's an example. Write this in the parser:

```
%{
struct parser_control
{
  int nastiness;
  int randomness;
};

#define YYPARSE_PARAM parm
%}
```

Then call the parser like this:

```
struct parser_control
{
  int nastiness;
  int randomness;
};
```

. . .

```
{
  struct parser_control foo;
  ...  /* Store proper data in foo.  */
  value = yyparse ((void *) &foo);
  ...
}
```

In the grammar actions, use expressions like this to refer to the data:

```
((struct parser_control *) parm)->randomness
```

If you wish to pass the additional parameter data to yylex, define the macro YYLEX_PARAM just like YYPARSE_PARAM, as shown here:

```
%{
struct parser_control
{
  int nastiness;
  int randomness;
};

#define YYPARSE_PARAM parm
#define YYLEX_PARAM parm
%}
```

You should then define yylex to accept one additional argument—the value of parm. (This makes either two or three arguments in total, depending on whether an argument of type YYLTYPE is passed.) You can declare the argument as a pointer to the proper object type, or you can declare it as void * and access the contents as shown above.

You can use '%pure_parser' to request a reentrant parser without also using YYPARSE_PARAM. Then you should call yyparse with no arguments, as usual.

4.3 The Error Reporting Function yyerror

The Bison parser detects a *parse error* or *syntax error* whenever it reads a token which cannot satisfy any syntax rule. An action in the grammar can also explicitly proclaim an error, using the macro YYERROR (see Section 4.4 [Special Features for Use in Actions], page 56).

The Bison parser expects to report the error by calling an error reporting function named yyerror, which you must supply. It is called by yyparse whenever a syntax error is found, and it receives one argument. For a parse error, the string is normally "parse error".

If you define the macro YYERROR_VERBOSE in the Bison declarations section (see Section 3.1.2 [The Bison Declarations Section], page 35), then Bison provides a more verbose and specific error message string instead of just plain `"parse error"`. It doesn't matter what definition you use for YYERROR_VERBOSE, just whether you define it.

The parser can detect one other kind of error: stack overflow. This happens when the input contains constructions that are very deeply nested. It isn't likely you will encounter this, since the Bison parser extends its stack automatically up to a very large limit. But if overflow happens, yyparse calls yyerror in the usual fashion, except that the argument string is `"parser stack overflow"`.

The following definition suffices in simple programs:

```
yyerror (s)
     char *s;
{
  fprintf (stderr, "%s\n", s);
}
```

After yyerror returns to yyparse, the latter will attempt error recovery if you have written suitable error recovery grammar rules (see Chapter 6 [Error Recovery], page 71). If recovery is impossible, yyparse will immediately return 1.

The variable yynerrs contains the number of syntax errors encountered so far. Normally this variable is global; but if you request a pure parser (see Section 3.6.7 [A Pure (Reentrant) Parser], page 48) then it is a local variable which only the actions can access.

4.4 Special Features for Use in Actions

Here is a table of Bison constructs, variables and macros that are useful in actions.

'$$'   Acts like a variable that contains the semantic value for the grouping made by the current rule. See Section 3.5.3 [Actions], page 40.

'$n'   Acts like a variable that contains the semantic value for the nth component of the current rule. See Section 3.5.3 [Actions], page 40.

'$<typealt>$'
             Like $$ but specifies alternative typealt in the union specified by the %union declaration. See Section 3.5.4 [Data Types of Values in Actions], page 42.

'$<typealt>n'
             Like $n but specifies alternative typealt in the union specified by the %union declaration. See Section 3.5.4 [Data Types of Values in Actions], page 42.

'YYABORT;'
>   Return immediately from **yyparse**, indicating failure. See Section 4.1 [The Parser Function **yyparse**], page 51.

'YYACCEPT;'
>   Return immediately from **yyparse**, indicating success. See Section 4.1 [The Parser Function **yyparse**], page 51.

'YYBACKUP (*token*, *value*);'
>   Unshift a token. This macro is allowed only for rules that reduce a single value, and only when there is no look-ahead token. It installs a look-ahead token with token type *token* and semantic value *value*; then it discards the value that was going to be reduced by this rule.
>
>   If the macro is used when it is not valid, such as when there is a look-ahead token already, then it reports a syntax error with a message 'cannot back up' and performs ordinary error recovery.
>
>   In either case, the rest of the action is not executed.

'YYEMPTY'   Value stored in **yychar** when there is no look-ahead token.

'YYERROR;'
>   Cause an immediate syntax error. This statement initiates error recovery just as if the parser itself had detected an error; however, it does not call **yyerror**, and does not print any message. If you want to print an error message, call **yyerror** explicitly before the 'YYERROR;' statement. See Chapter 6 [Error Recovery], page 71.

'YYRECOVERING'
>   This macro stands for an expression that has the value 1 when the parser is recovering from a syntax error, and 0 the rest of the time. See Chapter 6 [Error Recovery], page 71.

'yychar'   Variable containing the current look-ahead token. (In a pure parser, this is actually a local variable within **yyparse**.) When there is no look-ahead token, the value YYEMPTY is stored in the variable. See Section 5.1 [Look-Ahead Tokens], page 59.

'yyclearin;'
>   Discard the current look-ahead token. This is useful primarily in error rules. See Chapter 6 [Error Recovery], page 71.

'yyerrok;'
>   Resume generating error messages immediately for subsequent syntax errors. This is useful primarily in error rules. See Chapter 6 [Error Recovery], page 71.

'@*n*'   Acts like a structure variable containing information on the line numbers and column numbers of the *n*th component of the current rule. The structure has four members, like this:

```
struct {
  int first_line, last_line;
  int first_column, last_column;
};
```

Thus, to get the starting line number of the third component, you would use '@3.first_line'.

In order for the members of this structure to contain valid information, you must make **yylex** supply this information about each token. If you need only certain members, then **yylex** need only fill in those members.

The use of this feature makes the parser noticeably slower.

5 The Bison Parser Algorithm

As Bison reads tokens, it pushes them onto a stack along with their semantic values. The stack is called the *parser stack*. Pushing a token is traditionally called *shifting*.

For example, suppose the infix calculator has read '1 + 5 *', with a '3' to come. The stack will have four elements, one for each token that was shifted.

But the stack does not always have an element for each token read. When the last *n* tokens and groupings shifted match the components of a grammar rule, they can be combined according to that rule. This is called *reduction*. Those tokens and groupings are replaced on the stack by a single grouping whose symbol is the result (left hand side) of that rule. Running the rule's action is part of the process of reduction, because this is what computes the semantic value of the resulting grouping.

For example, if the infix calculator's parser stack contains this:

```
1 + 5 * 3
```

and the next input token is a newline character, then the last three elements can be reduced to 15 via the rule:

```
expr: expr '*' expr;
```

Then the stack contains just these three elements:

```
1 + 15
```

At this point, another reduction can be made, resulting in the single value 16. Then the newline token can be shifted.

The parser tries, by shifts and reductions, to reduce the entire input down to a single grouping whose symbol is the grammar's start-symbol (see Section 1.1 [Languages and Context-Free Grammars], page 13).

This kind of parser is known in the literature as a bottom-up parser.

5.1 Look-Ahead Tokens

The Bison parser does *not* always reduce immediately as soon as the last *n* tokens and groupings match a rule. This is because such a simple strategy is inadequate to handle most languages. Instead, when a reduction is possible, the parser sometimes "looks ahead" at the next token in order to decide what to do.

When a token is read, it is not immediately shifted; first it becomes the *look-ahead token*, which is not on the stack. Now the parser can perform one or more reductions of tokens and groupings on the stack, while the look-ahead token remains off to the side. When no more reductions should take place, the look-ahead token is shifted onto the stack. This does not mean that all possible reductions have been done; depending on the token type of the look-ahead token, some rules may choose to delay their application.

Here is a simple case where look-ahead is needed. These three rules define expressions which contain binary addition operators and postfix unary factorial operators ('!'), and allow parentheses for grouping.

```
expr:     term '+' expr
        | term
        ;

term:     '(' expr ')'
        | term '!'
        | NUMBER
        ;
```

Suppose that the tokens '1 + 2' have been read and shifted; what should be done? If the following token is ')', then the first three tokens must be reduced to form an **expr**. This is the only valid course, because shifting the ')' would produce a sequence of symbols **term ')'**, and no rule allows this.

If the following token is '!', then it must be shifted immediately so that '2 !' can be reduced to make a **term**. If instead the parser were to reduce before shifting, '1 + 2' would become an **expr**. It would then be impossible to shift the '!' because doing so would produce on the stack the sequence of symbols **expr '!'**. No rule allows that sequence.

The current look-ahead token is stored in the variable **yychar**. See Section 4.4 [Special Features for Use in Actions], page 56.

5.2 Shift/Reduce Conflicts

Suppose we are parsing a language which has if-then and if-then-else statements, with a pair of rules like this:

```
if_stmt:
          IF expr THEN stmt
        | IF expr THEN stmt ELSE stmt
        ;
```

Here we assume that **IF**, **THEN** and **ELSE** are terminal symbols for specific keyword tokens.

When the **ELSE** token is read and becomes the look-ahead token, the contents of the stack (assuming the input is valid) are just right for reduction by the first rule. But it is also legitimate to shift the **ELSE**, because that would lead to eventual reduction by the second rule.

This situation, where either a shift or a reduction would be valid, is called a *shift/reduce conflict*. Bison is designed to resolve these conflicts by choosing to shift, unless otherwise directed by operator precedence declarations. To see the reason for this, let's contrast it with the other alternative.

Since the parser prefers to shift the **ELSE**, the result is to attach the else-clause to the innermost if-statement, making these two inputs equivalent:

```
if x then if y then win (); else lose;
```

```
if x then do; if y then win (); else lose; end;
```

But if the parser chose to reduce when possible rather than shift, the result would be to attach the else-clause to the outermost if-statement, making these two inputs equivalent:

```
if x then if y then win (); else lose;
```

```
if x then do; if y then win (); end; else lose;
```

The conflict exists because the grammar as written is ambiguous: either parsing of the simple nested if-statement is legitimate. The established convention is that these ambiguities are resolved by attaching the else-clause to the innermost if-statement; this is what Bison accomplishes by choosing to shift rather than reduce. (It would ideally be cleaner to write an unambiguous grammar, but that is very hard to do in this case.) This particular ambiguity was first encountered in the specifications of Algol 60 and is called the "dangling else" ambiguity.

To avoid warnings from Bison about predictable, legitimate shift/reduce conflicts, use the %expect n declaration. There will be no warning as long as the number of shift/reduce conflicts is exactly n. See Section 3.6.5 [Suppressing Conflict Warnings], page 47.

The definition of if_stmt above is solely to blame for the conflict, but the conflict does not actually appear without additional rules. Here is a complete Bison input file that actually manifests the conflict:

```
%token IF THEN ELSE variable
%%
stmt:       expr
        | if_stmt
        ;

if_stmt:
            IF expr THEN stmt
        | IF expr THEN stmt ELSE stmt
        ;

expr:       variable
        ;
```

5.3 Operator Precedence

Another situation where shift/reduce conflicts appear is in arithmetic expressions. Here shifting is not always the preferred resolution; the Bison declarations for operator precedence allow you to specify when to shift and when to reduce.

5.3.1 When Precedence is Needed

Consider the following ambiguous grammar fragment (ambiguous because
the input '1 - 2 * 3' can be parsed in two different ways):

```
expr:       expr '-' expr
      | expr '*' expr
      | expr '<' expr
      | '(' expr ')'
      ...
      ;
```

Suppose the parser has seen the tokens '1', '-' and '2'; should it reduce them
via the rule for the subtraction operator? It depends on the next token. Of
course, if the next token is ')', we must reduce; shifting is invalid because no
single rule can reduce the token sequence '- 2)' or anything starting with
that. But if the next token is '*' or '<', we have a choice: either shifting or
reduction would allow the parse to complete, but with different results.

To decide which one Bison should do, we must consider the results. If
the next operator token *op* is shifted, then it must be reduced first in order
to permit another opportunity to reduce the difference. The result is (in
effect) '1 - (2 *op* 3)'. On the other hand, if the subtraction is reduced
before shifting *op*, the result is '(1 - 2) *op* 3'. Clearly, then, the choice of
shift or reduce should depend on the relative precedence of the operators '-'
and *op*: '*' should be shifted first, but not '<'.

What about input such as '1 - 2 - 5'; should this be '(1 - 2) - 5' or
should it be '1 - (2 - 5)'? For most operators we prefer the former, which
is called *left association*. The latter alternative, *right association*, is desirable
for assignment operators. The choice of left or right association is a matter
of whether the parser chooses to shift or reduce when the stack contains
'1 - 2' and the look-ahead token is '-': shifting makes right-associativity.

5.3.2 Specifying Operator Precedence

Bison allows you to specify these choices with the operator precedence
declarations %left and %right. Each such declaration contains a list of
tokens, which are operators whose precedence and associativity is being declared. The %left declaration makes all those operators left-associative and
the %right declaration makes them right-associative. A third alternative is
%nonassoc, which declares that it is a syntax error to find the same operator
twice "in a row".

The relative precedence of different operators is controlled by the order
in which they are declared. The first %left or %right declaration in the file
declares the operators whose precedence is lowest, the next such declaration
declares the operators whose precedence is a little higher, and so on.

5.3.3 Precedence Examples

In our example, we would want the following declarations:

```
%left '<'
%left '-'
%left '*'
```

In a more complete example, which supports other operators as well, we would declare them in groups of equal precedence. For example, '+' is declared with '-':

```
%left '<' '>' '=' NE LE GE
%left '+' '-'
%left '*' '/'
```

(Here NE and so on stand for the operators for "not equal" and so on. We assume that these tokens are more than one character long and therefore are represented by names, not character literals.)

5.3.4 How Precedence Works

The first effect of the precedence declarations is to assign precedence levels to the terminal symbols declared. The second effect is to assign precedence levels to certain rules: each rule gets its precedence from the last terminal symbol mentioned in the components. (You can also specify explicitly the precedence of a rule. See Section 5.4 [Context-Dependent Precedence], page 63.)

Finally, the resolution of conflicts works by comparing the precedence of the rule being considered with that of the look-ahead token. If the token's precedence is higher, the choice is to shift. If the rule's precedence is higher, the choice is to reduce. If they have equal precedence, the choice is made based on the associativity of that precedence level. The verbose output file made by '-v' (see Chapter 9 [Invoking Bison], page 79) says how each conflict was resolved.

Not all rules and not all tokens have precedence. If either the rule or the look-ahead token has no precedence, then the default is to shift.

5.4 Context-Dependent Precedence

Often the precedence of an operator depends on the context. This sounds outlandish at first, but it is really very common. For example, a minus sign typically has a very high precedence as a unary operator, and a somewhat lower precedence (lower than multiplication) as a binary operator.

The Bison precedence declarations, %left, %right and %nonassoc, can only be used once for a given token; so a token has only one precedence declared in this way. For context-dependent precedence, you need to use an additional mechanism: the %prec modifier for rules.

The %prec modifier declares the precedence of a particular rule by specifying a terminal symbol whose precedence should be used for that rule. It's
not necessary for that symbol to appear otherwise in the rule. The modifier's
syntax is:

%prec *terminal-symbol*

and it is written after the components of the rule. Its effect is to assign
the rule the precedence of *terminal-symbol*, overriding the precedence that
would be deduced for it in the ordinary way. The altered rule precedence
then affects how conflicts involving that rule are resolved (see Section 5.3
[Operator Precedence], page 61).

Here is how %prec solves the problem of unary minus. First, declare a
precedence for a fictitious terminal symbol named UMINUS. There are no
tokens of this type, but the symbol serves to stand for its precedence:

```
...
%left '+' '-'
%left '*'
%left UMINUS
```

Now the precedence of UMINUS can be used in specific rules:

```
exp:    ...
    | exp '-' exp
    ...
    | '-' exp %prec UMINUS
```

5.5 Parser States

The function yyparse is implemented using a finite-state machine. The
values pushed on the parser stack are not simply token type codes; they
represent the entire sequence of terminal and nonterminal symbols at or
near the top of the stack. The current state collects all the information
about previous input which is relevant to deciding what to do next.

Each time a look-ahead token is read, the current parser state together
with the type of look-ahead token are looked up in a table. This table entry
can say, "Shift the look-ahead token." In this case, it also specifies the new
parser state, which is pushed onto the top of the parser stack. Or it can
say, "Reduce using rule number n." This means that a certain number of
tokens or groupings are taken off the top of the stack, and replaced by one
grouping. In other words, that number of states are popped from the stack,
and one new state is pushed.

There is one other alternative: the table can say that the look-ahead token
is erroneous in the current state. This causes error processing to begin (see
Chapter 6 [Error Recovery], page 71).

5.6 Reduce/Reduce Conflicts

A reduce/reduce conflict occurs if there are two or more rules that apply to the same sequence of input. This usually indicates a serious error in the grammar.

For example, here is an erroneous attempt to define a sequence of zero or more **word** groupings.

```
sequence: /* empty */
                { printf ("empty sequence\n"); }
        | maybeword
        | sequence word
                { printf ("added word %s\n", $2); }
        ;

maybeword: /* empty */
                { printf ("empty maybeword\n"); }
        | word
                { printf ("single word %s\n", $1); }
        ;
```

The error is an ambiguity: there is more than one way to parse a single **word** into a **sequence**. It could be reduced to a **maybeword** and then into a **sequence** via the second rule. Alternatively, nothing-at-all could be reduced into a **sequence** via the first rule, and this could be combined with the **word** using the third rule for **sequence**.

There is also more than one way to reduce nothing-at-all into a **sequence**. This can be done directly via the first rule, or indirectly via **maybeword** and then the second rule.

You might think that this is a distinction without a difference, because it does not change whether any particular input is valid or not. But it does affect which actions are run. One parsing order runs the second rule's action; the other runs the first rule's action and the third rule's action. In this example, the output of the program changes.

Bison resolves a reduce/reduce conflict by choosing to use the rule that appears first in the grammar, but it is very risky to rely on this. Every reduce/reduce conflict must be studied and usually eliminated. Here is the proper way to define **sequence**:

```
sequence: /* empty */
                { printf ("empty sequence\n"); }
        | sequence word
                { printf ("added word %s\n", $2); }
        ;
```

Here is another common error that yields a reduce/reduce conflict:

```
sequence: /* empty */
        | sequence words
```

```
            | sequence redirects
            ;

  words:    /* empty */
          | words word
          ;

  redirects:/* empty */
          | redirects redirect
          ;
```

The intention here is to define a sequence which can contain either **word** or **redirect** groupings. The individual definitions of **sequence**, **words** and **redirects** are error-free, but the three together make a subtle ambiguity: even an empty input can be parsed in infinitely many ways!

Consider: nothing-at-all could be a **words**. Or it could be two **words** in a row, or three, or any number. It could equally well be a **redirects**, or two, or any number. Or it could be a **words** followed by three **redirects** and another **words**. And so on.

Here are two ways to correct these rules. First, to make it a single level of sequence:

```
  sequence: /* empty */
          | sequence word
          | sequence redirect
          ;
```

Second, to prevent either a **words** or a **redirects** from being empty:

```
  sequence: /* empty */
          | sequence words
          | sequence redirects
          ;

  words:    word
          | words word
          ;

  redirects:redirect
          | redirects redirect
          ;
```

5.7 Mysterious Reduce/Reduce Conflicts

Sometimes reduce/reduce conflicts can occur that don't look warranted. Here is an example:

```
%token ID

%%
def:      param_spec return_spec ','
          ;
param_spec:
                  type
          |       name_list ':' type
          ;
return_spec:
                  type
          |       name ':' type
          ;
type:     ID
          ;
name:     ID
          ;
name_list:
                  name
          |       name ',' name_list
          ;
```

It would seem that this grammar can be parsed with only a single token of
look-ahead: when a **param_spec** is being read, an **ID** is a **name** if a comma or
colon follows, or a **type** if another **ID** follows. In other words, this grammar
is LR(1).

However, Bison, like most parser generators, cannot actually handle all
LR(1) grammars. In this grammar, two contexts, that after an **ID** at the
beginning of a **param_spec** and likewise at the beginning of a **return_spec**,
are similar enough that Bison assumes they are the same. They appear
similar because the same set of rules would be active—the rule for reducing
to a **name** and that for reducing to a **type**. Bison is unable to determine
at that stage of processing that the rules would require different look-ahead
tokens in the two contexts, so it makes a single parser state for them both.
Combining the two contexts causes a conflict later. In parser terminology,
this occurrence means that the grammar is not LALR(1).

In general, it is better to fix deficiencies than to document them. But
this particular deficiency is intrinsically hard to fix; parser generators that
can handle LR(1) grammars are hard to write and tend to produce parsers
that are very large. In practice, Bison is more useful as it is now.

When the problem arises, you can often fix it by identifying the two
parser states that are being confused, and adding something to make them
look distinct. In the above example, adding one rule to **return_spec** as
follows makes the problem go away:

```
%token BOGUS
...
%%
...
return_spec:
        type
      | name ':' type
      /* This rule is never used. */
      | ID BOGUS
      ;
```

This corrects the problem because it introduces the possibility of an additional active rule in the context after the ID at the beginning of return_spec. This rule is not active in the corresponding context in a param_spec, so the two contexts receive distinct parser states. As long as the token BOGUS is never generated by yylex, the added rule cannot alter the way actual input is parsed.

In this particular example, there is another way to solve the problem: rewrite the rule for return_spec to use ID directly instead of via name. This also causes the two confusing contexts to have different sets of active rules, because the one for return_spec activates the altered rule for return_spec rather than the one for name.

```
param_spec:
        type
      | name_list ':' type
      ;
return_spec:
        type
      | ID ':' type
      ;
```

5.8 Stack Overflow, and How to Avoid It

The Bison parser stack can overflow if too many tokens are shifted and not reduced. When this happens, the parser function yyparse returns a nonzero value, pausing only to call yyerror to report the overflow.

By defining the macro YYMAXDEPTH, you can control how deep the parser stack can become before a stack overflow occurs. Define the macro with a value that is an integer. This value is the maximum number of tokens that can be shifted (and not reduced) before overflow. It must be a constant expression whose value is known at compile time.

The stack space allowed is not necessarily allocated. If you specify a large value for YYMAXDEPTH, the parser actually allocates a small stack at first, and then makes it bigger by stages as needed. This increasing allocation happens automatically and silently. Therefore, you do not need to make YYMAXDEPTH painfully small merely to save space for ordinary inputs that do not need much stack.

The default value of `YYMAXDEPTH`, if you do not define it, is 10000.

You can control how much stack is allocated initially by defining the macro `YYINITDEPTH`. This value too must be a compile-time constant integer. The default is 200.

6 Error Recovery

It is not usually acceptable to have a program terminate on a parse error. For example, a compiler should recover sufficiently to parse the rest of the input file and check it for errors; a calculator should accept another expression.

In a simple interactive command parser where each input is one line, it may be sufficient to allow yyparse to return 1 on error and have the caller ignore the rest of the input line when that happens (and then call yyparse again). But this is inadequate for a compiler, because it forgets all the syntactic context leading up to the error. A syntax error deep within a function in the compiler input should not cause the compiler to treat the following line like the beginning of a source file.

You can define how to recover from a syntax error by writing rules to recognize the special token error. This is a terminal symbol that is always defined (you need not declare it) and reserved for error handling. The Bison parser generates an error token whenever a syntax error happens; if you have provided a rule to recognize this token in the current context, the parse can continue.

For example:

```
stmnts:  /* empty string */
       | stmnts '\n'
       | stmnts exp '\n'
       | stmnts error '\n'
```

The fourth rule in this example says that an error followed by a newline makes a valid addition to any stmnts.

What happens if a syntax error occurs in the middle of an exp? The error recovery rule, interpreted strictly, applies to the precise sequence of a stmnts, an error and a newline. If an error occurs in the middle of an exp, there will probably be some additional tokens and subexpressions on the stack after the last stmnts, and there will be tokens to read before the next newline. So the rule is not applicable in the ordinary way.

But Bison can force the situation to fit the rule, by discarding part of the semantic context and part of the input. First it discards states and objects from the stack until it gets back to a state in which the error token is acceptable. (This means that the subexpressions already parsed are discarded, back to the last complete stmnts.) At this point the error token can be shifted. Then, if the old look-ahead token is not acceptable to be shifted next, the parser reads tokens and discards them until it finds a token which is acceptable. In this example, Bison reads and discards input until the next newline so that the fourth rule can apply.

The choice of error rules in the grammar is a choice of strategies for error recovery. A simple and useful strategy is simply to skip the rest of the current input line or current statement if an error is detected:

```
stmnt: error ';'   /* on error, skip until ';' is read */
```

It is also useful to recover to the matching close-delimiter of an opening-delimiter that has already been parsed. Otherwise the close-delimiter will probably appear to be unmatched, and generate another, spurious error message:

```
primary:  '(' expr ')'
        | '(' error ')'
        ...
        ;
```

Error recovery strategies are necessarily guesses. When they guess wrong, one syntax error often leads to another. In the above example, the error recovery rule guesses that an error is due to bad input within one **stmnt**. Suppose that instead a spurious semicolon is inserted in the middle of a valid **stmnt**. After the error recovery rule recovers from the first error, another syntax error will be found straightaway, since the text following the spurious semicolon is also an invalid **stmnt**.

To prevent an outpouring of error messages, the parser will output no error message for another syntax error that happens shortly after the first; only after three consecutive input tokens have been successfully shifted will error messages resume.

Note that rules which accept the **error** token may have actions, just as any other rules can.

You can make error messages resume immediately by using the macro **yyerrok** in an action. If you do this in the error rule's action, no error messages will be suppressed. This macro requires no arguments; 'yyerrok;' is a valid C statement.

The previous look-ahead token is reanalyzed immediately after an error. If this is unacceptable, then the macro **yyclearin** may be used to clear this token. Write the statement 'yyclearin;' in the error rule's action.

For example, suppose that on a parse error, an error handling routine is called that advances the input stream to some point where parsing should once again commence. The next symbol returned by the lexical scanner is probably correct. The previous look-ahead token ought to be discarded with 'yyclearin;'.

The macro **YYRECOVERING** stands for an expression that has the value 1 when the parser is recovering from a syntax error, and 0 the rest of the time. A value of 1 indicates that error messages are currently suppressed for new syntax errors.

7 Handling Context Dependencies

The Bison paradigm is to parse tokens first, then group them into larger syntactic units. In many languages, the meaning of a token is affected by its context. Although this violates the Bison paradigm, certain techniques (known as *kludges*) may enable you to write Bison parsers for such languages.

(Actually, "kludge" means any technique that gets its job done but is neither clean nor robust.)

7.1 Semantic Info in Token Types

The C language has a context dependency: the way an identifier is used depends on what its current meaning is. For example, consider this:

```
foo (x);
```

This looks like a function call statement, but if `foo` is a typedef name, then this is actually a declaration of `x`. How can a Bison parser for C decide how to parse this input?

The method used in GNU C is to have two different token types, `IDENTIFIER` and `TYPENAME`. When `yylex` finds an identifier, it looks up the current declaration of the identifier in order to decide which token type to return: `TYPENAME` if the identifier is declared as a typedef, `IDENTIFIER` otherwise.

The grammar rules can then express the context dependency by the choice of token type to recognize. `IDENTIFIER` is accepted as an expression, but `TYPENAME` is not. `TYPENAME` can start a declaration, but `IDENTIFIER` cannot. In contexts where the meaning of the identifier is *not* significant, such as in declarations that can shadow a typedef name, either `TYPENAME` or `IDENTIFIER` is accepted—there is one rule for each of the two token types.

This technique is simple to use if the decision of which kinds of identifiers to allow is made at a place close to where the identifier is parsed. But in C this is not always so: C allows a declaration to redeclare a typedef name provided an explicit type has been specified earlier:

```
typedef int foo, bar, lose;
static foo (bar);        /* redeclare bar as static variable */
static int foo (lose);   /* redeclare foo as function */
```

Unfortunately, the name being declared is separated from the declaration construct itself by a complicated syntactic structure—the "declarator".

As a result, part of the Bison parser for C needs to be duplicated, with all the nonterminal names changed: once for parsing a declaration in which a typedef name can be redefined, and once for parsing a declaration in which that can't be done. Here is a part of the duplication, with actions omitted for brevity:

```
initdcl:
```

```
            declarator maybeasm '='
            init
          | declarator maybeasm
          ;

   notype_initdcl:
            notype_declarator maybeasm '='
            init
          | notype_declarator maybeasm
          ;
```

Here `initdcl` can redeclare a typedef name, but `notype_initdcl` cannot. The distinction between `declarator` and `notype_declarator` is the same sort of thing.

There is some similarity between this technique and a lexical tie-in (described next), in that information which alters the lexical analysis is changed during parsing by other parts of the program. The difference is here the information is global, and is used for other purposes in the program. A true lexical tie-in has a special-purpose flag controlled by the syntactic context.

7.2 Lexical Tie-ins

One way to handle context-dependency is the *lexical tie-in*: a flag which is set by Bison actions, whose purpose is to alter the way tokens are parsed.

For example, suppose we have a language vaguely like C, but with a special construct '`hex` (*hex-expr*)'. After the keyword `hex` comes an expression in parentheses in which all integers are hexadecimal. In particular, the token '`a1b`' must be treated as an integer rather than as an identifier if it appears in that context. Here is how you can do it:

```
%{
int hexflag;
%}
%%
...
expr:     IDENTIFIER
        | constant
        | HEX '('
                { hexflag = 1; }
          expr ')'
                { hexflag = 0;
                  $$ = $4; }
        | expr '+' expr
                { $$ = make_sum ($1, $3); }
        ...
        ;
```

```
constant:
            INTEGER
          | STRING
          ;
```

Here we assume that `yylex` looks at the value of `hexflag`; when it is nonzero, all integers are parsed in hexadecimal, and tokens starting with letters are parsed as integers if possible.

The declaration of `hexflag` shown in the C declarations section of the parser file is needed to make it accessible to the actions (see Section 3.1.1 [The C Declarations Section], page 35). You must also write the code in `yylex` to obey the flag.

7.3 Lexical Tie-ins and Error Recovery

Lexical tie-ins make strict demands on any error recovery rules you have. See Chapter 6 [Error Recovery], page 71.

The reason for this is that the purpose of an error recovery rule is to abort the parsing of one construct and resume in some larger construct. For example, in C-like languages, a typical error recovery rule is to skip tokens until the next semicolon, and then start a new statement, like this:

```
stmt:   expr ';'
      | IF '(' expr ')' stmt { ... }
      ...
      error ';'
                { hexflag = 0; }
      ;
```

If there is a syntax error in the middle of a 'hex (*expr*)' construct, this error rule will apply, and then the action for the completed 'hex (*expr*)' will never run. So `hexflag` would remain set for the entire rest of the input, or until the next `hex` keyword, causing identifiers to be misinterpreted as integers.

To avoid this problem the error recovery rule itself clears `hexflag`.

There may also be an error recovery rule that works within expressions. For example, there could be a rule which applies within parentheses and skips to the close-parenthesis:

```
expr:   ...
      | '(' expr ')'
                { $$ = $2; }
      | '(' error ')'
      ...
```

If this rule acts within the `hex` construct, it is not going to abort that construct (since it applies to an inner level of parentheses within the construct). Therefore, it should not clear the flag: the rest of the **hex** construct should be parsed with the flag still in effect.

What if there is an error recovery rule which might abort out of the **hex** construct or might not, depending on circumstances? There is no way you can write the action to determine whether a **hex** construct is being aborted or not. So if you are using a lexical tie-in, you had better make sure your error recovery rules are not of this kind. Each rule must be such that you can be sure that it always will, or always won't, have to clear the flag.

8 Debugging Your Parser

If a Bison grammar compiles properly but doesn't do what you want when it runs, the `yydebug` parser-trace feature can help you figure out why.

To enable compilation of trace facilities, you must define the macro `YYDEBUG` when you compile the parser. You could use '-DYYDEBUG=1' as a compiler option or you could put '#define YYDEBUG 1' in the C declarations section of the grammar file (see Section 3.1.1 [The C Declarations Section], page 35). Alternatively, use the '-t' option when you run Bison (see Chapter 9 [Invoking Bison], page 79). We always define `YYDEBUG` so that debugging is always possible.

The trace facility uses `stderr`, so you must add `#include <stdio.h>` to the C declarations section unless it is already there.

Once you have compiled the program with trace facilities, the way to request a trace is to store a nonzero value in the variable `yydebug`. You can do this by making the C code do it (in `main`, perhaps), or you can alter the value with a C debugger.

Each step taken by the parser when `yydebug` is nonzero produces a line or two of trace information, written on `stderr`. The trace messages tell you these things:

- Each time the parser calls `yylex`, what kind of token was read.

- Each time a token is shifted, the depth and complete contents of the state stack (see Section 5.5 [Parser States], page 64).

- Each time a rule is reduced, which rule it is, and the complete contents of the state stack afterward.

To make sense of this information, it helps to refer to the listing file produced by the Bison '-v' option (see Chapter 9 [Invoking Bison], page 79). This file shows the meaning of each state in terms of positions in various rules, and also what each state will do with each possible input token. As you read the successive trace messages, you can see that the parser is functioning according to its specification in the listing file. Eventually you will arrive at the place where something undesirable happens, and you will see which parts of the grammar are to blame.

The parser file is a C program and you can use C debuggers on it, but it's not easy to interpret what it is doing. The parser function is a finite-state machine interpreter, and aside from the actions it executes the same code over and over. Only the values of variables show where in the grammar it is working.

The debugging information normally gives the token type of each token read, but not its semantic value. You can optionally define a macro named `YYPRINT` to provide a way to print the value. If you define `YYPRINT`, it should take three arguments. The parser will pass a standard I/O stream, the numeric code for the token type, and the token value (from `yylval`).

Here is an example of YYPRINT suitable for the multi-function calculator (see Section 2.4.1 [Declarations for mfcalc], page 28):

```
#define YYPRINT(file, type, value)    yyprint (file, type, value)

static void
yyprint (file, type, value)
     FILE *file;
     int type;
     YYSTYPE value;
{
  if (type == VAR)
    fprintf (file, " %s", value.tptr->name);
  else if (type == NUM)
    fprintf (file, " %d", value.val);
}
```

9 Invoking Bison

The usual way to invoke Bison is as follows:

    bison infile

Here *infile* is the grammar file name, which usually ends in '.y'. The parser file's name is made by replacing the '.y' with '.tab.c'. Thus, the 'bison foo.y' filename yields 'foo.tab.c', and the 'bison hack/foo.y' filename yields 'hack/foo.tab.c'.

9.1 Bison Options

Bison supports both traditional single-letter options and mnemonic long option names. Long option names are indicated with '--' instead of '-'. Abbreviations for option names are allowed as long as they are unique. When a long option takes an argument, like '--file-prefix', connect the option name and the argument with '='.

Here is a list of options that can be used with Bison, alphabetized by short option. It is followed by a cross key alphabetized by long option.

'-b *file-prefix*'
'--file-prefix=*prefix*'

> Specify a prefix to use for all Bison output file names. The names are chosen as if the input file were named '*prefix*.c'.

'-d'
'--defines'

> Write an extra output file containing macro definitions for the token type names defined in the grammar and the semantic value type YYSTYPE, as well as a few **extern** variable declarations.
>
> If the parser output file is named '*name*.c' then this file is named '*name*.h'.
>
> This output file is essential if you wish to put the definition of yylex in a separate source file, because yylex needs to be able to refer to token type codes and the variable yylval. See Section 4.2.2 [Semantic Values of Tokens], page 53.

'-l'
'--no-lines'

> Don't put any #line preprocessor commands in the parser file. Ordinarily Bison puts them in the parser file so that the C compiler and debuggers will associate errors with your source file, the grammar file. This option causes them to associate errors with the parser file, treating it as an independent source file in its own right.

'-n'
'--no-parser'

> Do not include any C code in the parser file; generate tables only. The parser file contains just #define directives and static variable declarations.
>
> This option also tells Bison to write the C code for the grammar actions into a file named 'filename.act', in the form of a brace-surrounded body fit for a switch statement.

'-o outfile'
'--output-file=outfile'

> Specify the name outfile for the parser file.
>
> The other output files' names are constructed from outfile as described under the '-v' and '-d' options.

'-p prefix'
'--name-prefix=prefix'

> Rename the external symbols used in the parser so that they start with prefix instead of 'yy'. The precise list of symbols renamed is yyparse, yylex, yyerror, yynerrs, yylval, yychar and yydebug.
>
> For example, if you use '-p c', the names become cparse, clex, and so on.
>
> See Section 3.7 [Multiple Parsers in the Same Program], page 50.

'-r'
'--raw'   Pretend that %raw was specified. See Section 3.6.8 [Decl Summary], page 48.

'-t'
'--debug'   Output a definition of the macro YYDEBUG into the parser file, so that the debugging facilities are compiled. See Chapter 8 [Debugging Your Parser], page 77.

'-v'
'--verbose'

> Write an extra output file containing verbose descriptions of the parser states and what is done for each type of look-ahead token in that state.
>
> This file also describes all the conflicts, both those resolved by operator precedence and the unresolved ones.
>
> The file's name is made by removing '.tab.c' or '.c' from the parser output file name, and adding '.output' instead.
>
> Therefore, if the input file is 'foo.y', then the parser file is called 'foo.tab.c' by default. As a consequence, the verbose output file is called 'foo.output'.

'-V'
'--version'
>   Print the version number of Bison and exit.

'-h'
'--help'   Print a summary of the command-line options to Bison and exit.

'-y'
'--yacc'
'--fixed-output-files'
>   Equivalent to '-o y.tab.c'; the parser output file is called
>   'y.tab.c', and the other outputs are called 'y.output' and
>   'y.tab.h'. The purpose of this option is to imitate Yacc's out-
>   put file name conventions. Thus, the following shell script can
>   substitute for Yacc:
>
>   bison -y $*

9.2 Environment Variables

Here is a list of environment variables which affect the way Bison runs.

'BISON_SIMPLE'
'BISON_HAIRY'
>   Much of the parser generated by Bison is copied verbatim from
>   a file called 'bison.simple'. If Bison cannot find that file, or
>   if you would like to direct Bison to use a different copy, setting
>   the environment variable BISON_SIMPLE to the path of the file
>   will cause Bison to use that copy instead.
>
>   When the '%semantic_parser' delcaration is used, Bison copies
>   from a file called 'bison.hairy' instead. The location of this
>   file can also be specified or overridden in a similar fashion, with
>   the BISON_HAIRY environment variable.

9.3 Option Cross Key

Here is a list of options, alphabetized by long option, to help you find the
corresponding short option.

```
--debug      . . . . . . . . . . . . . . . . . . . . . . . .  -t
--defines    . . . . . . . . . . . . . . . . . . . . . . . .  -d
--file-prefix  . . . . . . . . . . . . . . . . . . . . . . .  -b
--fixed-output-files . . . . . . . . . . . . . . . . . . . .  -y
--help . . . . . . . . . . . . . . . . . . . . . . . . . . .  -h
--name-prefix  . . . . . . . . . . . . . . . . . . . . . . .  -p
--no-lines . . . . . . . . . . . . . . . . . . . . . . . . .  -l
--no-parser  . . . . . . . . . . . . . . . . . . . . . . . .  -n
--output-file  . . . . . . . . . . . . . . . . . . . . . . .  -o
```

```
--raw      . . . . . . . . . . . . . . . . . . . . . . . . -r
--token-table  . . . . . . . . . . . . . . . . . . . . . -k
--verbose  . . . . . . . . . . . . . . . . . . . . . . . -v
--version  . . . . . . . . . . . . . . . . . . . . . . . -V
--yacc . . . . . . . . . . . . . . . . . . . . . . . . . -y
```

9.4 Invoking Bison under VMS

The command line syntax for Bison on VMS is a variant of the usual Bison command syntax—adapted to fit VMS conventions.

To find the VMS equivalent for any Bison option, start with the long option, and substitute a '/' for the leading '--', and substitute a '_' for each '-' in the name of the long option. For example, the following invocation under VMS:

```
bison /debug/name_prefix=bar foo.y
```

is equivalent to the following command under POSIX.

```
bison --debug --name-prefix=bar foo.y
```

The VMS file system does not permit filenames such as 'foo.tab.c'. In the above example, the output file would instead be named 'foo_tab.c'.

Appendix A Bison Symbols

error   A token name reserved for error recovery. This token may be
                used in grammar rules so as to allow the Bison parser to rec-
                ognize an error in the grammar without halting the process.
                In effect, a sentence containing an error may be recognized as
                valid. On a parse error, the token **error** becomes the current
                look-ahead token. Actions corresponding to **error** are then ex-
                ecuted, and the look-ahead token is reset to the token that orig-
                inally caused the violation. See Chapter 6 [Error Recovery],
                page 71.

YYABORT   Macro to pretend that an unrecoverable syntax error has oc-
                curred, by making **yyparse** return 1 immediately. The error
                reporting function **yyerror** is not called. See Section 4.1 [The
                Parser Function **yyparse**], page 51.

YYACCEPT   Macro to pretend that a complete utterance of the language
                has been read, by making **yyparse** return 0 immediately. See
                Section 4.1 [The Parser Function **yyparse**], page 51.

YYBACKUP   Macro to discard a value from the parser stack and fake a look-
                ahead token. See Section 4.4 [Special Features for Use in Ac-
                tions], page 56.

YYERROR   Macro to pretend that a syntax error has just been detected: call
                yyerror and then perform normal error recovery if possible (see
                Chapter 6 [Error Recovery], page 71), or (if recovery is impos-
                sible) make **yyparse** return 1. See Chapter 6 [Error Recovery],
                page 71.

YYERROR_VERBOSE
                Macro that you define with **#define** in the Bison declarations
                section to request verbose, specific error message strings when
                yyerror is called.

YYINITDEPTH
                Macro for specifying the initial size of the parser stack. See
                Section 5.8 [Stack Overflow], page 68.

YYLEX_PARAM
                Macro for specifying an extra argument (or list of extra argu-
                ments) for **yyparse** to pass to **yylex**. See Section 4.2.4 [Calling
                Conventions for Pure Parsers], page 54.

YYLTYPE   Macro for the data type of **yylloc**; a structure with four mem-
                bers. See Section 4.2.3 [Textual Positions of Tokens], page 53.

yyltype   Default value for YYLTYPE.

`YYMAXDEPTH`
> Macro for specifying the maximum size of the parser stack. See Section 5.8 [Stack Overflow], page 68.

`YYPARSE_PARAM`
> Macro for specifying the name of a parameter that `yyparse` should accept. See Section 4.2.4 [Calling Conventions for Pure Parsers], page 54.

`YYRECOVERING`
> Macro whose value indicates whether the parser is recovering from a syntax error. See Section 4.4 [Special Features for Use in Actions], page 56.

`YYSTYPE`   Macro for the data type of semantic values; `int` by default. See Section 3.5.1 [Data Types of Semantic Values], page 40.

`yychar`   External integer variable that contains the integer value of the current look-ahead token. (In a pure parser, it is a local variable within `yyparse`.) Error-recovery rule actions may examine this variable. See Section 4.4 [Special Features for Use in Actions], page 56.

`yyclearin`
> Macro used in error-recovery rule actions. It clears the previous look-ahead token. See Chapter 6 [Error Recovery], page 71.

`yydebug`   External integer variable set to zero by default. If `yydebug` is given a nonzero value, the parser will output information on input symbols and parser action. See Chapter 8 [Debugging Your Parser], page 77.

`yyerrok`   Macro to cause parser to recover immediately to its normal mode after a parse error. See Chapter 6 [Error Recovery], page 71.

`yyerror`   User-supplied function to be called by `yyparse` on error. The function receives one argument, a pointer to a character string containing an error message. See Section 4.3 [The Error Reporting Function `yyerror`], page 55.

`yylex`   User-supplied lexical analyzer function, called with no arguments to get the next token. See Section 4.2 [The Lexical Analyzer Function `yylex`], page 51.

`yylval`   External variable in which `yylex` should place the semantic value associated with a token. (In a pure parser, it is a local variable within `yyparse` and its address is passed to `yylex`.) See Section 4.2.2 [Semantic Values of Tokens], page 53.

`yylloc`   External variable in which `yylex` should place the line and column numbers associated with a token. (In a pure parser, it is a local variable within `yyparse`, and its address is passed to

yylex.) You can ignore this variable if you don't use the '@' feature in the grammar actions. See Section 4.2.3 [Textual Positions of Tokens], page 53.

yynerrs   Global variable which Bison increments each time there is a parse error. (In a pure parser, it is a local variable within **yyparse.**) See Section 4.3 [The Error Reporting Function **yyerror**], page 55.

yyparse   The parser function produced by Bison; call this function to start parsing. See Section 4.1 [The Parser Function **yyparse**], page 51.

%left   Bison declaration to assign left associativity to token(s). See Section 3.6.2 [Operator Precedence], page 46.

%no_lines
           Bison declaration to avoid generating **#line** directives in the parser file. See Section 3.6.8 [Decl Summary], page 48.

%nonassoc
           Bison declaration to assign nonassociativity to token(s). See Section 3.6.2 [Operator Precedence], page 46.

%prec   Bison declaration to assign a precedence to a specific rule. See Section 5.4 [Context-Dependent Precedence], page 63.

%pure_parser
           Bison declaration to request a pure (reentrant) parser. See Section 3.6.7 [A Pure (Reentrant) Parser], page 48.

%raw   Bison declaration to use Bison internal token code numbers in token tables instead of the usual Yacc-compatible token code numbers. See Section 3.6.8 [Decl Summary], page 48.

%right   Bison declaration to assign right associativity to token(s). See Section 3.6.2 [Operator Precedence], page 46.

%start   Bison declaration to specify the start symbol. See Section 3.6.6 [The Start-Symbol], page 48.

%token   Bison declaration to declare token(s) without specifying precedence. See Section 3.6.1 [Token Type Names], page 45.

%token_table
           Bison declaration to include a token name table in the parser file. See Section 3.6.8 [Decl Summary], page 48.

%type   Bison declaration to declare nonterminals. See Section 3.6.4 [Nonterminal Symbols], page 47.

%union   Bison declaration to specify several possible data types for semantic values. See Section 3.6.3 [The Collection of Value Types], page 46.

These are the punctuation and delimiters used in Bison input:

'%%'   Delimiter used to separate the grammar rule section from the Bison declarations section or the additional C code section. See Section 1.7 [The Overall Layout of a Bison Grammar], page 18.

'%{ %}'   All code listed between '%{' and '%}' is copied directly to the output file uninterpreted. Such code forms the "C declarations" section of the input file. See Section 3.1 [Outline of a Bison Grammar], page 35.

'/*...*/'   Comment delimiters, as in C.

':'   Separates a rule's result from its components. See Section 3.3 [Syntax of Grammar Rules], page 38.

';'   Terminates a rule. See Section 3.3 [Syntax of Grammar Rules], page 38.

'|'   Separates alternate rules for the same result nonterminal. See Section 3.3 [Syntax of Grammar Rules], page 38.

Appendix B Glossary

Backus-Naur Form (BNF)
: Formal method of specifying context-free grammars. BNF was first used in the *ALGOL-60* report, 1963. See Section 1.1 [Languages and Context-Free Grammars], page 13.

Context-free grammars
: Grammars specified as rules that can be applied regardless of context. Thus, if there is a rule which says that an integer can be used as an expression, integers are allowed *anywhere* an expression is permitted. See Section 1.1 [Languages and Context-Free Grammars], page 13.

Dynamic allocation
: Allocation of memory that occurs during execution, rather than at compile time or on entry to a function.

Empty string
: Analogous to the empty set in set theory, the empty string is a character string of length zero.

Finite-state stack machine
: A "machine" that has discrete states in which it is said to exist at each instant in time. As input to the machine is processed, the machine moves from state to state as specified by the logic of the machine. In the case of the parser, the input is the language being parsed, and the states correspond to various stages in the grammar rules. See Chapter 5 [The Bison Parser Algorithm], page 59.

Grouping
: A language construct that is (in general) grammatically divisible; for example, 'expression' or 'declaration' in C. See Section 1.1 [Languages and Context-Free Grammars], page 13.

Infix operator
: An arithmetic operator that is placed between the operands on which it performs some operation.

Input stream
: A continuous flow of data between devices or programs.

Language construct
: One of the typical usage schemas of the language. For example, one of the constructs of the C language is the `if` statement. See Section 1.1 [Languages and Context-Free Grammars], page 13.

Left associativity
: Operators having left associativity are analyzed from left to right: 'a+b+c' first computes 'a+b' and then combines with 'c'. See Section 5.3 [Operator Precedence], page 61.

Left recursion

A rule whose result symbol is also its first component symbol; for example, 'expseq1 : expseq1 ',' exp;'. See Section 3.4 [Recursive Rules], page 39.

Left-to-right parsing

Parsing a sentence of a language by analyzing it token by token from left to right. See Chapter 5 [The Bison Parser Algorithm], page 59.

Lexical analyzer (scanner)

A function that reads an input stream and returns tokens one by one. See Section 4.2 [The Lexical Analyzer Function `yylex`], page 51.

Lexical tie-in

A flag, set by actions in the grammar rules, which alters the way tokens are parsed. See Section 7.2 [Lexical Tie-ins], page 74.

Literal string token

A token which consists of two or more fixed characters. See Section 3.2 [Symbols], page 36.

Look-ahead token

A token already read but not yet shifted. See Section 5.1 [Look-Ahead Tokens], page 59.

LALR(1)   The class of context-free grammars that Bison (like most other parser generators) can handle; a subset of LR(1). See Section 5.7 [Mysterious Reduce/Reduce Conflicts], page 66.

LR(1)   The class of context-free grammars in which at most one token of look-ahead is needed to disambiguate the parsing of any piece of input.

Nonterminal symbol

A grammar symbol standing for a grammatical construct that can be expressed through rules in terms of smaller constructs; in other words, a construct that is not a token. See Section 3.2 [Symbols], page 36.

Parse error

An error encountered during parsing of an input stream due to invalid syntax. See Chapter 6 [Error Recovery], page 71.

Parser   A function that recognizes valid sentences of a language by analyzing the syntax structure of a set of tokens passed to it from a lexical analyzer.

Postfix operator

An arithmetic operator that is placed after the operands upon which it performs some operation.

Reduction   Replacing a string of nonterminals and/or terminals with a single
             nonterminal, according to a grammar rule. See Chapter 5 [The
             Bison Parser Algorithm], page 59.

Reentrant   A reentrant subprogram is a subprogram which can be in invoked
             any number of times in parallel, without interference between
             the various invocations. See Section 3.6.7 [A Pure (Reentrant)
             Parser], page 48.

Reverse polish notation
             A language in which all operators are postfix operators.

Right recursion
             A rule whose result symbol is also its last component symbol; for
             example, 'expseq1: exp ',' expseq1;'. See Section 3.4 [Recur-
             sive Rules], page 39.

Semantics   In computer languages, the semantics are specified by the actions
             taken for each instance of the language, i.e., the meaning of
             each statement. See Section 3.5 [Defining Language Semantics],
             page 40.

Shift   A parser is said to shift when it makes the choice of analyzing
             further input from the stream rather than reducing immediately
             some already-recognized rule. See Chapter 5 [The Bison Parser
             Algorithm], page 59.

Single-character literal
             A single character that is recognized and interpreted as is. See
             Section 1.2 [From Formal Rules to Bison Input], page 14.

Start symbol
             The nonterminal symbol that stands for a complete valid utter-
             ance in the language being parsed. The start symbol is usually
             listed as the first nonterminal symbol in a language specification.
             See Section 3.6.6 [The Start-Symbol], page 48.

Symbol table
             A data structure where symbol names and associated data are
             stored during parsing to allow for recognition and use of existing
             information in repeated uses of a symbol. See Section 2.4 [Multi-
             function Calc], page 28.

Token   A basic, grammatically indivisible unit of a language. The sym-
             bol that describes a token in the grammar is a terminal symbol.
             The input of the Bison parser is a stream of tokens which comes
             from the lexical analyzer. See Section 3.2 [Symbols], page 36.

Terminal symbol
             A grammar symbol that has no rules in the grammar and there-
             fore is grammatically indivisible. The piece of text it represents

is a token. See Section 1.1 [Languages and Context-Free Grammars], page 13.

Index

$

$$ 40
$*n* 40

%

%expect 47
%left 62
%nonassoc 62
%prec 63
%pure_parser 48
%right 62
%start 48
%token 45
%type 47
%union 46

@

@*n* 57

|

| 38

A

action 40
action data types 42
action features summary 56
actions in mid-rule 42
actions, semantic 16
additional C code section 36
algorithm of parser 59
associativity 62

B

Backus-Naur form 13
Bison declaration summary 48
Bison declarations 44
Bison declarations (introduction) ... 35

Bison grammar 14
Bison invocation 79
Bison parser 16
Bison parser algorithm 59
Bison symbols, table of 83
Bison utility 16
BISON_HAIRY 81
BISON_SIMPLE 81
BNF 13

C

C code, section for additional 36
C declarations section 35
C-language interface 51
calc 25
calculator, infix notation 25
calculator, multi-function 28
calculator, simple 19
character token 36
compiling the parser 25
conflicts 60
conflicts, reduce/reduce 65
conflicts, suppressing warnings of .. 47
context-dependent precedence 63
context-free grammar 13
controlling function 24

D

dangling else 60
data types in actions 42
data types of semantic values 40
debugging 77
declaration summary 48
declarations, Bison 44
declarations, Bison (introduction) .. 35
declarations, C 35
declaring literal string tokens 45
declaring operator precedence 46
declaring the start symbol 48
declaring token type names 45

declaring value types 46
declaring value types, nonterminals 47
default action 41
default data type 40
default stack limit 69
default start symbol 48
defining language semantics 40

E

else, dangling 60
environment variables 81
error 71
error recovery 71
error recovery, simple 27
error reporting function 55
error reporting routine 24
examples, simple 19
exercises 34

F

file format 18
finite-state machine 64
formal grammar 14
format of grammar file 18

G

glossary 87
grammar file 18
grammar rule syntax 38
grammar rules section 35
grammar, Bison 14
grammar, context-free 13
grouping, syntactic 13

I

infix notation calculator 25
interface 51
introduction 1

invoking Bison 79
invoking Bison under VMS 82

L

LALR(1) 67
language semantics, defining 40
layout of Bison grammar 18
left recursion 39
lexical analyzer 51
lexical analyzer, purpose 16
lexical analyzer, writing 22
lexical tie-in 74
literal string token 37
literal token 36
look-ahead token 59
LR(1) 67

M

main function in simple example 24
mfcalc 28
mid-rule actions 42
multi-function calculator 28
multicharacter literal 37
mutual recursion 39

N

nonterminal symbol 36

O

operator precedence 61
operator precedence, declaring 46
options for invoking Bison 79
overflow of parser stack 68

P

parse error 55
parser. 16
parser stack 59
parser stack overflow 68
parser state 64
polish notation calculator. 19
precedence declarations. 46
precedence of operators. 61
precedence, context-dependent 63
precedence, unary operator 63
preventing warnings about conflicts . . . 47
pure parser 48

R

recovery from errors 71
recursive rule 39
reduce/reduce conflict 65
reduction 59
reentrant parser 48
reverse polish notation 19
right recursion 39
`rpcalc` 19
rule syntax 38
rules section for grammar. 35
running Bison (introduction) 24

S

semantic actions 16
semantic value. 15
semantic value type 40
shift/reduce conflicts 60
shifting 59
simple examples 19
single-character literal 36
stack overflow 68
stack, parser. 59
stages in using Bison 17
start symbol. 14
start symbol, declaring 48

state (of parser) 64
string token 37
summary, action features 56
summary, Bison declaration. 48
suppressing conflict warnings 47
symbol. 36
symbol table example 30
symbols (abstract) 13
symbols in Bison, table of 83
syntactic grouping 13
syntax error 55
syntax of grammar rules. 38

T

terminal symbol 36
token 13
token type 36
token type names, declaring 45
tracing the parser 77

U

unary operator precedence. 63
using Bison. 17

V

value type, semantic 40
value types, declaring 46
value types, nonterminals, declaring . . . 47
value, semantic 15
VMS 82

W

warnings, preventing 47
writing a lexical analyzer 22

Y

YYABORT............................. 51
YYACCEPT............................ 51
YYBACKUP............................ 57
yychar............................... 60
yyclearin........................... 72
yydebug............................. 77
YYDEBUG............................. 77
YYEMPTY............................. 57
yyerrok............................. 72
yyerror............................. 55
YYERROR............................. 57

YYERROR_VERBOSE 55
YYINITDEPTH 69
yylex............................... 51
YYLEX_PARAM 55
yylloc.............................. 53
YYLTYPE............................. 53
yylval.............................. 53
YYMAXDEPTH 68
yynerrs............................. 56
yyparse............................. 51
YYPARSE_PARAM 54
YYPRINT............................. 77
YYRECOVERING 72

Available from the Free Software Foundation..

This is a list of items available from the Free Software Foundation as of the publication of this manual. New items may not yet appear on this list. Please consult our web site at http://www.gnu.org/order/orders.html for current information and pricing, or call our distribution office at +1-617-542-5942.

BOOKS:

- **GNU Emacs Manual** - Using Emacs for editing. 518 pp. $30
- **GNU Emacs Lisp Reference Manual** - over 950 pp. $60
- **Programming in Emacs Lisp: An Introduction** - 257 pp. $20
- **Using and Porting GNU CC** - Compiler for C and more. 574 pp. $50
- **Debugging with GDB** - How to use the GNU Debugger. 201 pp. $20
- **GNU Make** - Extensions, writing makefiles, reference. 158 pp. $20
- **Bison Manual** - YACC-compatible parser generator. 104 pp. $20
- **GAWK: GNU Awk User's Guide** - Easy text processing. 324 pp. $25
- **Texinfo** - Producing printed and online documentation. 256 pp. $25
- **C Library Reference Manual** - Revised for V.2. 2 vol., 1080 pp. $50
- **Flex: The Lexical Scanner Generator** - An improved lex. 120 pp. $20
- **Termcap Manual** - Display terminal data base library. 64 pp. $15
- **Calc Manual** - Numeric math and algebra in GNU Emacs. 572 pp. $50

OTHER ITEMS:

- **GNU Source Code CD-ROM** All the GNU project source code - 3 discs.
- **GNU Compiler Tools Binaries CD-ROM** Directly installable compiler executables for several operating systems (see *http://www.gnu.org*).
- **GNU Software for MS-Windows and MS-DOS and Compatible Systems** - the GNU compiler, tools, and utilities for various Microsoft OSes and compatible systems. This CD-ROM comes with a printed guide to installation.
- **Reference cards** - available for Emacs, Calc, GDB, Flex, and Bison.
- **GNU t-shirts**

All purchases made from the FSF help support the development of more free software and documentation. The Free Software Foundation is a 501 (c) 3 not-for-profit corporation, and donations are tax-deductible in the U.S.

Free Software Foundation, 59 Temple Place, Suite 330, Boston, MA 02111
+1-617-542-5942 Fax: +1-617-542-2652 gnu@gnu.org http://www.gnu.org